JOURNEY
to my
FAITH

Family Devotional Series

*Helping Parents Develop Their
Children's Love for God and for People*

VOLUME 2

DAVID IBRAHIM

ANM
publishers

JOURNEY to my FAITH

VOLUME 2

Paperback ISBN: 978-1-946174-06-2

Published by:

Advancing Native Missions
P.O. Box 5303
Charlottesville, VA 22905
www.AdvancingNativeMissions.com

Graphic Design by:
Christopher Kirk, GraphicsForSuccess.com

DEDICATION

Firstly, I take a great opportunity to acknowledge our Lord Jesus Christ for using this empty vessel for His glory.

Secondly, I dedicate this book to my father, who was my spiritual hero and a servant of God, Pastor James W. G. (November 29, 1927 - May 26, 2015). Also to my mother Mrs. Parveen A. G. (October 20, 1933 - April 19, 2017) a godly woman, who has a great hand in my upbringing. Both of them were godly couple, who were great inspiration to all their seven children and their spouses, as well as to their twenty one grand-children, eleven great-grand children, and also tens of thousands to whom they served passionately as their humble shepherds for over sixty years.

ACKNOWLEDGEMENT

I take this great opportunity to acknowledge and thank our Lord Jesus Christ for using this broken vessel for His glory.

As John Donne (1572–1631) said, "No man is an island…" It's amazing how, at times, the Lord puts a certain vision in our lives and brings people along the way in order to accomplish it. We, being in the "body of Christ", need one another. I don't have the words to describe my deepest gratitude, for Ms. Faye Boyd, who put in hours and hours to check the script thoroughly on each page. Ms. Boyd, thank you so much for your patience and willingness to make it possible.

I appreciate Ms. Janet Shaffer and Mr. Tommy Meche, Pastor Richard Cohen, and Annlyn Ouzts, who wholeheartedly brought the work to the next level by checking and correcting any typographical inaccuracies. Also I am grateful for Mr. Paulo R. Gill's services in research efforts, and lastly, but most importantly, for my dear wife, our children and other concerned friends, who kept encouraging and sharing new ideas to make this project possible.

CONTENTS

INTRODUCTION

And these words which I command you today shall be in your heart. ⁷You shall teach them diligently to your children, and shall talk of them when you sit in your house, when you walk by the way, when you lie down, and when you rise up. ⁸You shall bind them as a sign on your hand, and they shall be as frontlets between your eyes." (Deuteronomy 6:6-8)

Answering Your Biggest Question from Vol. 1 & My Challenge to You

After the publication of Volume 1 of *Journey to My Faith*, the one question I have been asked most is, "Why have you included quotations from people who are not Christians?" This is a good and valid question because, as believers in Jesus, we should always live and speak what is true and right. This especially is so when God blesses us with children and has given us the responsibility to raise them in a godly manner. So let me explain to you why I have included quotations from people who do not believe in Jesus Christ for salvation.

First, let's talk about where truth comes from. If you were to ask believers where they think truth comes from, most would probably say that it comes from the Bible. That is all well and good, except there are things we know to be true that are not mentioned in the Bible. For instance, many of our math principles, like '2+2=4' or the quadratic equation, are true but are not mentioned in the Bible. There are also many scientific discoveries that are true. Plenty of times, some of those discoveries are interpreted incorrectly, evolution being a good example of that. However, when it comes to the ones that are true, the Bible has, directly or indirectly, mentioned only some of those, but not all of them.

Does that mean those math principles and scientific discoveries are less true than the truth that we learn in the Bible that says there is only one God, or that salvation comes through faith in Jesus Christ alone? It comes down to this. All truth is not mentioned in the Bible, but all truth is from God. More specifically, truth is defined by the character of God because God is truth (Deuteronomy 32:3,4; John 14:6; 15:26; 16:13). Before there was anything material or immaterial, God was. Truth, just like everything else, finds its origin in God Himself.

How do we know that murder is wrong? It is because God is life and because man is made in the image of God. Therefore, to take a life without just cause is wrong. We know that just cause could include self-defense, capital punishment, or war, but God says in the Ten Commandments, "You shall not murder" (Exodus 20:13). He tells us this because God is life. You can go through everything that is truth, and it will point back to one or more aspects of God's character because truth is defined by who God is.

The question then remains—are people who do not have their faith in Jesus Christ for salvation and therefore are not made alive in Christ unfit to speak or share truth? Let's look at this more closely. All human beings are made in the image of God, saved or unsaved (Genesis 1:26). The Bible talks about how God has put eternity in each person's heart (Ecclesiastes 3:11). I believe this includes a capability to discern God-defined truth. But since Adam chose to sin in the Garden of Eden, all human beings have a sinful nature because we are all descendants from Adam (Romans 5:12-14). This sin problem is in all of us. Does that sin nature totally nullify the capacity of discerning and speaking truth that comes from being in the image of God? If that were true, then salvation for any of us would not be possible because the Holy Spirit would try to convict us of our sin to lead to us salvation (John 16:7-11), but we would not be able to understand. There has to be a level of capacity to understand truth, even in our fallen, sinful state.

Our role as parents is one of discernment. This is true from the start of God blessing us with our children. From the things they watch, see, read, and hear, we should filter the information that is presented to our children. In some cases, that means totally censoring the information. In others, it means turning that into a teachable moment with discussion while we allow the information to be presented. As good parents, we should control these things for our kids until they get to a point where they can make these decisions properly on their own. What the world presents should always be approached with much caution, but it is not totally deprived of truth. At the same time, even when it comes to those people we trust as strong spiritual leaders in our life, we as parents should be discerning to make sure what is communicated is in line with the Word of God. It is just as possible for a saved person to speak untruth as it is for an unsaved person to speak truth. The believers in Berea acted on this responsibility even when the Apostle Paul preached in their midst (Acts 17:10, 11). If it is important to examine what Paul said, then it is our responsibility to double check what our spiritual leaders teach us against the Word of God, and we should be doing this with everything that is presented to our families.

My encouragement to you as parents is that, when you get to the end of each daily devotion in *Journey to My Faith*, be discerning with the quotes. Use them as discussion points with your kids. Talk with your children about whether what is quoted is truth and look to Scripture to verify it. If you as parents are unsure yourselves, make it a family project to search out the Bible for truth and compare God's truth with that quote.

The Need

The lessons are focused and based on The Holy Bible, so that the children will learn with understanding the purpose why the Savior came for all mankind. This only could be experienced by knowing God's Word and having a personal relationship with His Son. This is the very heart of Jesus Christ that shall not perish (John 3:16).

Just as children grow physically, they also need spiritual nourishment, on a daily basis, to grow in their faith. Research has concluded that in the early stages of growth, children have the capability to absorb anything taught to them, like a sponge. This leaves a lasting impact on them for the rest of their lives.

We have seen the discipline Muslims parents have, for making sure that the children will go to the Mosque or Madrassa (Islamic school) on a daily basis. The effort behind this is to educate them with the core of Islamic faith, and for the children to memorize the whole Quran. This concept is an honor for the family, and it roots the children firm in their faith, till death. On daily basis, Muslims parents are determined to set aside one or two hours for their children to focus on their religious values and teachings.

In America or Europe, generally children attend public/government schools for 6-7 hours daily, 5 days a week, 10 months each year for the length of 12 years. Christian parents don't always have an option to implement a Christian worldview. Competing worldview is here, and subtle to imprint its on our children. Unfortunately, in our society, 90% of our children are being educated by the very system that is itself the problem. Those forces who have rejected, and have completely eliminated Biblical principals from their schools, now have embraced evolution. Therefore, this is a time of urgency. We need to be on fire for the Lord, and realize that our children are our mission field. We as Christians are not called to "fit in," but to "stand out."

Parents' Responsibility

Since the Lord has blessed us with such a wonderful gift of parenthood, we make sure to do our best to take care of children's physical needs like clothing, schooling and food. However, the question is, who is accountable to fulfill that "Spiritual Gap"? It is our responsibility to fill the void in the lives of our children, who are our Mission field. Many parents have the misconception that it's the responsibility of the "Sunday School" teachers to teach their children about Biblical values and heritage. Just 30-45 minutes a week are not enough for spiritual grooming. Rather, as parents, it's your everyday duty as Scripture commands us:

> *"This Book of the Law shall not depart from your mouth, but you shall meditate in it day and night that you may observe to do according to all that is written in it. For then you will make your way prosperous, and then you will have good success." (Joshua 1:8)*

I am humbled to share that the Lord planted a seed in my heart, to work on a daily Bible study for the families with school-aged children. The vision began when I started traveling back and forth to Pakistan. During that time duration, I met many parents who showed concern for the spiritual growth of their children. Although parents want to guide their children, they are unable to do so thoroughly and systematically, due to the lack of Biblical material that captures children's interest.

The concept of Sunday school, in third world countries, is entirely different from that in the West, where it's mostly organized according to age. However, in developing countries, due to limited space in the church building, children of all ages are accommodated in one room. The lesson is generalized from kindergarten to higher grades, therefore only major Biblical stories are taught repeatedly. The writer's desire is that this workbook will be translated into other major languages, and be circulated as an outreach tool around the world, to indigenous church groups.

Being a parent of growing children myself, this thought truly stirred my heart with a burden: that it's our responsibility to raise our children in the fear of the Lord on a daily basis at home. According to the research done and penned in the book titled *Already Gone*, by Mr. Ken Ham and his co-writers, the shocking survey result was that only 11% of the children after high school return to the church. Where are we as parents failing to do our part? Why do 89% of our children want nothing to do with Christianity anymore? This has puzzled me, and thus, after prayerfully seeking God's wisdom, the Lord gave me the vision that resulted in the birth of this workbook: *Journey to My Faith*.

Methodology

Each lesson is planned, not only to help your children, but also to help you, as a parent, learn about the basic Biblical truths. Also, much time was dedicated to gathering all the general information that makes these lessons interesting. The intention of the writer is not to overwhelm the children, although on some days you will read more than 30 Bible verses, which focus on one thought for that specific day.

End Results

The purpose of this journal is not to merely promote religious facts, but rather the Biblical and Spiritual depth of Christianity. It is a daily Bible study for the whole family, studying from Genesis through Revelation. The children will know, chronologically, the theme, purpose and synopsis of each book of the Bible, along with the number of chapters in each book. Each week, the children will memorize one or two Bible verses expressing the main foundation of our Christian faith. Also, the focus is on the Biblical method of evangelism, which is not based on any denomination or para-church organization, but solely on the foundation of Biblical Truth. Furthermore, reading the amazing stories of great men and women of the Bible, whom God chose, will also broaden children's understanding about who the God of Abraham, Isaac and Jacob really is, and His characteristics and attributes found both in the Old and New Testaments.

Simultaneously, children will increase their general knowledge about each country, learning fascinating facts about different areas, and their global impact. They will learn about inventions, and read quotes of great men and women, who have wholeheartedly contributed to the welfare and improvement of humanity, in the fields of geography, mathematics, medicine, politics, philosophy, science, and technology. Additionally, the short weekly tests and reviews will help you evaluate what your children have studied.

As you assist your children in gaining the spiritual truths through this book, children will realize that God is more than able to use His people mightily for His glory, as long as we allow Him to work in our lives, with humility and submission. I have great confidence that one day, by God's grace, your children's names will be included in the fields of future discoveries and inventions that will benefit humanity. Primarily, though, it is important that they will be soul winners for the Lord in the years to come.

It's my humble prayer that every day, as you go through these pages with your children, the Lord will be the source of your wisdom, strength, joy, and perseverance, revealing the insights of His mysteries and revelations to you. Most importantly, I pray that whatever you do or wherever you go as a family, you will be a sweet fragrance of Christ. Others can sense the Lord's presence and reverence in your life, in all the days to come.

> *So I close with a quote from Solomon, which personally has touched and transformed my inner being: "The fear of the Lord is the beginning of wisdom; and the knowledge of the holy is understanding." (Proverbs 9:10)*

Prayer Guidelines

I hope that you and your children will spend quality time in prayer, by observing Biblical principles, and by giving its ultimate importance in your daily lives.

What is Prayer?

It is communication with God, at anytime. The scriptures give some guidelines of how we are to pray. The Lord's Prayer has the complete pattern for us on how to pray...

> [5] *"And when you pray, you shall not be like the hypocrites. For they love to pray standing in the synagogues and on the corners of the streets, that they may be seen by men. Assuredly, I say to you, they have their reward.* [6] *But you, when you pray, go into your room, and when you have shut your door, pray to your Father who is in the secret place; and your Father who sees in secret will reward you openly.* [7] *And when you pray, do not use vain repetitions as the heathen do. For they think that they will be heard for their many words.* [8] *Therefore do not be like them. For your Father knows the things you have need of before you ask Him." (Matt 6:5-8)*

Ask

Although our Heavenly Father knows the things we need, we still should ask, for James tells us, *"You do not have because you do not ask."* (James 4:2-3) So it is crucial that we should keep asking, seeking and knocking. *"So I say to you, ask, and it will be given to you; seek, and you will find; knock, and it will be opened to you."* (Luke 11:9) *"Casting all your care upon Him, for He cares for you."* (1 Peter 5:7) This should comfort you as you consider the challenges and needs of you and your family. Remember that your spiritual responsibility is to daily bathe your loved ones in prayer, for their future destiny can be preserved by your prayers for them.

Intercede

The word "intercede" means, "to intervene on behalf of another." Hebrews 7:25 tells us that Jesus lives to make intercession for us. He is our Pattern, our Leader, and our Shepherd. If He is interceding for us, then we are surely called to intercede for others. Pray for those who burden your heart, or as the Holy Spirit directs you. While prayer can differ daily, intercession should be the centerpiece of prayer, not only for your family, but also for your friends, neighbors, colleagues, church, pastor, and national leaders, etc., especially for those who are nonbelievers in Jesus Christ. A very important point is that intercessory prayer takes place in the spiritual realm, where the battles are won or lost.

Speak Scriptures

During your prayer, it is very important to speak scripture verses to express that you "have faith in God." There are things we ask of God, but then He sometimes leads us to proclaim or declare things. (Mark 11:21-24) He clearly tells us that we can speak to the mountain under certain conditions and the mountains will be removed. When Satan tempts you to feel lonely, forgotten or even deserted, declare God's Word that assures you of His promise to bless and comfort you during difficult times. In order to do that, you must, *"Study to show thyself approved unto God."* (2 Tim. 2:15)

In your prayers speak God's Word over you, your family members, and friends. Remember those scriptural assurances that *"by His stripes, we are healed"* (Isaiah 53:5), *"All my needs are met according to His riches in glory by Christ Jesus"* (Philippians 4:19), and, most importantly, *"I can do all things through Christ who strengthens me"* (Philippians 4:13).

Repentance

Many of us understand the term "repentance" means "turning from sin." However, the biblical definition of "repent" means "to change one's mind." The Bible also tells us that true repentance will result in a change of actions (Luke 3:8-14; Acts 3:19). So, the full biblical definition of repentance is, a change of mind that results in a change of action. Acts 26:20 declares, *"I preached that they should repent and turn to God and prove their repentance by their deeds. For godly sorrow produces repentance leading to salvation, not to be regretted; but the sorrow of the world produces death."* (2 Corinthians 7:10)

The Lord tells us in Psalm 51:17 that He will not turn away a broken and contrite or repentant heart! He will not turn us away! God's Word clearly says that, if one hides iniquity in his heart, He will not hear him. (Psalm 66:18) So once you give Him thanks, praise and worship, your heart is open to confess your sins. When you've done this, you need to believe by faith that your sins truly are forgiven, and the result will be great inner peace. He not only forgives your sins, He will also enable you to resist leaning toward rebellion and independence, if you ask.

Enjoy His Presence

As you spend great quality time with Jesus, render unto Him praise and thanksgiving, and speak the Word, you will sense Him very near and will enjoy His presence.

During your prayer time, worship, read, meditate, and rejoice in a God who hears you when you call on His name. The scripture clearly assures us through the Words spoken to Jeremiah, *"For I know the thoughts that I think toward you, says the Lord, thoughts of peace and not of evil, to give you a future and a hope. [12] Then you will call upon Me and go and pray to Me, and I will listen to you. [13] And you will seek Me and find Me, when you search for Me with all your heart."* (Jeremiah 29.11-13)

While or when you focusing on God's provisions, mercies, and goodness He has brought into your life. He will fill you with the joy of His presence. Always have an attitude of praise and thanksgiving in whatever circumstances you experience, so that His grace will sustain you, and to make you victorious through His Cross. It's very important that your opening and closing prayer each day of the study be done with humility and openness of heart, thus this will render your prayer meaningful and genuine.

"The Lord bless you, and keep you: the Lord make his face to shine upon you, and be gracious unto you; The Lord lift up his countenance upon you, and give you peace." (Numbers 6:24)

"Your word is a lamp to my feet and a
light to my path."

Psalm 119:105

Day 1 ~ The Establishment of David's Throne

OPENING PRAYER
READ: 2nd Samuel 5:1-20

Then all the tribes...

1) What did the Israelites tell David at Hebron?_____

_____

2) How did the City of David come into existence?_____

_____

3) How old was David when he became king over Israel, and how long did he reign?_____

_____

Explore God's World

MEMORY VERSES:

Ezekiel 18:4 "Behold, all souls are Mine; the soul of the father, as well as the soul of the son is Mine; The soul who sins shall die."

Job 23:13 "But He is unique, and who can make Him change? And whatever His soul desires, that He does."

1ST CHRONICLES
The book does not specifically name its author. Traditionally, the book of 1st Chronicles was by Ezra.
PURPOSE
1st Chronicles covers mostly the same information as 1st & 2nd Samuel and 1st & 2nd Kings. It focuses more on the priestly aspect of the time period and was written after the exile to help those returning to Israel understand how to worship God. The history focused on the Southern Kingdom, the tribes of Judah, Benjamin, and Levi. These tribes tended to be more faithful to God.

For Your Information

FUN FACTS	9 LARGEST OCEANS & SEAS	IRAQ
1. The earliest known compass dates from the Han Dynasty (221-207 BC), in China. 2. Before the invention of the microscope, doctors didn't know that tiny parasites were the cause of many diseases.	1) Pacific Ocean 2) Atlantic Ocean 3) Indian Ocean 4) Arctic Ocean 5) South China Sea 6) Caribbean Sea 7) Mediterranean Sea 8) Bering Sea 9) Sea of Okhotsk	...is in the continent of Asia. Baghdad is the capital. Abraham was from Ur and Isaac's wife, Rebekah was from Nahor, both cities are located in Iraq. Additionally, according to legend, Iraq is the site of the Biblical Garden of Eden. The country is also very rich in petroleum.

GROUP DISCUSSION AND CLOSING PRAYER

"Nobody has ever measured, not even poets, how much the heart can hold."
Zelda Fitzgerald

Day 2 ~ The Removal of the Ark to Jerusalem

OPENING PRAYER
READ: 2nd Samuel 6:1-23

Again David gathered...

1) From where did David and his men bring up the ark of God? _____
_____

2) Where was the ark of God first placed? _____
_____

3) What did the daughter of Saul tell David, and what was his response? _____
_____
_____

Explore God's World

MEMORY VERSES:

Ezekiel 18:4 "Behold, all souls are Mine; the soul of the father, as well as the soul of the son is Mine; The soul who sins shall die."

Job 23:13 "But He is unique, and who can make Him change? And whatever His soul desires, that He does."

2ND CHRONICLES

The book does not specifically name its author. Traditionally, 2nd Chronicles was written by Ezra.

PURPOSE

2nd Chronicles covers mostly the same information as 1st & 2nd Samuel and 1st & 2nd Kings. The focus is more on the priestly aspect of the time period. 2nd Chronicles is essentially an evaluation of the nation's religious history.

For Your Information

FUN FACTS	9 LARGEST OCEANS & SEAS	IRELAND
1. There is a beach in the Vaadhoo Island, Maldives where a blue tide glows at night. 2. Silk was first made by the Chinese, about 4,000 years ago. Silk thread is made from the cocoon of the silkworm moth, whose caterpillar eats the leaves of the mulberry tree.	1) Pacific Ocean 2) Atlantic Ocean 3) Indian Ocean 4) Arctic Ocean 5) South China Sea 6) Caribbean Sea 7) Mediterranean Sea 8) Bering Sea 9) Sea of Okhotsk	...is in the continent of Europe. Dublin is the capital. It is the 3rd largest island in Europe and the 12th largest island on Earth. The country is famous for its Norman and Anglo-Irish castles. There are no snakes in Ireland. Only one reptile, the common lizard, is native to the island.

GROUP DISCUSSION AND CLOSING PRAYER

"Maybe that's why life is so precious. No rewind or fast forward...just patience and faith."

Cristina Marrero

Day 3 ~ The Establishment of Davidic Covenant

Now it came to...

1) What did David say to the prophet Nathan?_____
_____

2) What was the Lord's message, which Nathan delivered to David?_____
_____

3) What was David's response after hearing God's promise?_____
_____

Explore God's World

MEMORY VERSES:

Ezekiel 18:4 "Behold, all souls are Mine; the soul of the father, as well as the soul of the son is Mine; The soul who sins shall die."

Job 23:13 "But He is unique, and who can make Him change? And whatever His soul desires, that He does."

EZRA

The book does not specifically name its author. The tradition is that the prophet Ezra wrote the book of Ezra. It is interesting to note that once Ezra appears on the scene in chapter 7, the author of the book of Ezra switches from writing in the third person to first person. This would also lend credibility to Ezra being the author.

PURPOSE

Ezra is devoted to events occurring in the land of Israel at the time of the return from the Babylonian captivity and subsequent years, covering a period of approximately a century, beginning in 538 B.C. The emphasis in Ezra is on the rebuilding of the Temple. It contains extensive genealogical records, principally for establishing the claims to the priesthood on the part of the descendants of Aaron.

For Your Information

FUN FACTS	9 LARGEST OCEANS & SEAS	ISRAEL
1. There are more English words beginning with the letter "s" than with any other letter. 2. Zacharias Janssen was a Dutch lens-maker who invented the first compound microscope in 1595. A compound microscope has more than one lens.	1) Pacific Ocean 2) Atlantic Ocean 3) Indian Ocean 4) Arctic Ocean 5) South China Sea 6) Caribbean Sea 7) Mediterranean Sea 8) Bering Sea 9) Sea of Okhotsk	...is in the continent of Asia. Jerusalem is the capital. Israel is the only Jewish state in the world. It has the largest fleet of F-16 aircraft outside of the USA, the world's most impenetrable airline security, and is the world's largest wholesale diamond center. The Dead Sea, also known as the Salt Sea, is located here. Israel's dairy cows are the most productive in the world producing 12,000 liters of milk a year.

GROUP DISCUSSION AND CLOSING PRAYER

"The work that God does in us, when we wait, is usually more important than the thing for which we wait!"

Erwin W. Lutzer

Day 4 ~ The Conquest of David

OPENING PRAYER
READ: 2nd Samuel 8:1-18

After this it came...

1) Describe the battle between David and Hadad-ezer. _____

_____

_____

2) What happened to the Syrians of Damascus when they came to help Hadad-ezer? _____

_____

3) Who were David's officials? _____

_____

Explore God's World

MEMORY VERSES:

Ezekiel 18:4 "Behold, all souls are Mine; the soul of the father, as well as the soul of the son is Mine; The soul who sins shall die."

Job 23:13 "But He is unique, and who can make Him change? And whatever His soul desires, that He does."

NEHEMIAH

The book does not specifically name its author, but based on the fact that the Books of Ezra and Nehemiah were originally one, both Jewish and Christian traditions recognize Ezra as the author.

PURPOSE

Nehemiah is one of the history books, which continues the story of Israel's return from the Babylonian captivity and the rebuilding of the temple in Jerusalem.

For Your Information

FUN FACTS	9 LARGEST OCEANS & SEAS	ITALY
1. All Pakistani passports bears the inscription "this passport is valid for all countries of the world except Israel." 2. The first webcam was created in Cambridge University to check on the coffee level of a coffee pot.	1) Pacific Ocean 2) Atlantic Ocean 3) Indian Ocean 4) Arctic Ocean 5) South China Sea 6) Caribbean Sea 7) Mediterranean Sea 8) Bering Sea 9) Sea of Okhotsk	...is in the continent of Europe. Rome is the capital. Italy is famous for its fine food, elegance, opera, culture, and architecture, which includes the leaning tower of Pisa and the Roman Colosseum. Italy is the largest producer of fine wine in the world.

GROUP DISCUSSION AND CLOSING PRAYER

"Active faith gives thanks for a promise even though it is not yet performed, knowing that God's contracts are as good as cash."

Matthew Henry

Day 5 ~ David and Bathsheba

OPENING PRAYER
READ: 2nd Samuel 11:2-26 and 12:1-15

Then it happened...

1) Who was Bathsheba, and how she did become involved with David? _____
_____
_____

2) How was David responsible for Uriah's death? _____
_____

3) What was the Lord's message, which Nathan delivered to David? _____
_____

Explore God's World

MEMORY VERSES:

Ezekiel 18:4 "Behold, all souls are Mine; the soul of the father, as well as the soul of the son is Mine; The soul who sins shall die."

Job 23:13 "But He is unique, and who can make Him change? And whatever His soul desires, that He does."

ESTHER
The book does not specifically name its author. The most popular traditions suggest the author to be Mordecai (a major character in the book), or Ezra and Nehemiah, who would have also been familiar with Persian customs

PURPOSE
Esther was written to display the providence of God, especially in regard to His chosen people, Israel. Esther records the institution of the feast of Purim and the obligation of its perpetual observation. It was read at the feast of Purim to commemorate the great deliverance of the Jewish nation brought about by God through Esther. Jews today still read Esther during Purim.

For Your Information

FUN FACTS	9 LARGEST OCEANS & SEAS	JAMAICA
1. Tea bags were invented by Thomas Sullivan. The first bags were made from silk. 2. In New Zealand, it is illegal to name your kids the following names, "Fat Boy", "4real", "Cinderella Beauty Blossom", "Fish", and "Chips."	1) Pacific Ocean 2) Atlantic Ocean 3) Indian Ocean 4) Arctic Ocean 5) South China Sea 6) Caribbean Sea 7) Mediterranean Sea 8) Bering Sea 9) Sea of Okhotsk	...is in the continent of North America. Kingston is the capital. Reggae, ska, mento, dub, and dancehall music originated from here. Jamaica is famous for rum, and its rich nightlife attracts many tourists. The official language is English, and the most popular sport is cricket.

GROUP DISCUSSION AND CLOSING PRAYER

"What lies behind us and what lies before us are tiny matters compared to what lies within us."

Henry Haskins

Day 6 ~ Tamar and Amnon

OPENING PRAYER
READ: 2nd Samuel 13:1-29

After this Absalom...

1) How was Amnon related to Tamar? _____

_____

2) What advice did Jonadab give to Amnon? _____

_____

3) Why did Absalom kill Amnon? _____

_____

Explore God's World

MEMORY VERSES:

Ezekiel 18:4 "Behold, all souls are Mine; the soul of the father, as well as the soul of the son is Mine; The soul who sins shall die."

Job 23:13 "But He is unique, and who can make Him change? And whatever His soul desires, that He does."

JOB

Job does not specifically name its author. The most likely candidates are Job, Elihu, Moses, or Solomon.

PURPOSE

Job helps us to understand the following: Satan cannot bring financial and physical destruction upon us unless it is by God's permission. God has power over what Satan can and cannot do. It is beyond our human ability to understand the whys behind all the suffering in the world. We cannot always blame suffering on our lifestyles. Suffering may sometimes be allowed in our lives to purify, test, teach, or strengthen the soul. God, who is sufficient to meet our needs, requests and deserves our love and praise in all circumstances of life.

For Your Information

FUN FACTS	9 LARGEST OCEANS & SEAS	JAPAN
1. The Eiffel tower was originally intended for Barcelona, Spain but the project was rejected. 2. Contact lenses were invented and made in 1887 by Adolf Eugen Fick, the German physiologist. He first fitted animals with the lenses and then later made them for people.	1) Pacific Ocean 2) Atlantic Ocean 3) Indian Ocean 4) Arctic Ocean 5) South China Sea 6) Caribbean Sea 7) Mediterranean Sea 8) Bering Sea 9) Sea of Okhotsk	...is in the continent of Asia. Tokyo is the capital. Japan is famous for its hi tech and futuristic products, like the bullet trains and the cars they produce. The most famous car being the Toyota. The country is known for its origami art work, which is folded paper, and for its exotic foods such as sushi.

GROUP DISCUSSION AND CLOSING PRAYER

"O people of God, be great believers! Little faith will bring your souls to heaven, but great faith will bring heaven to your souls."

Charles H. Spurgeon

6   JOURNEY to my FAITH Family Devotional Series — VOLUME 2

Day 7 ~ Week in Review

MATCH THE FOLLOWING

_____ a.	Easter	1. Ezra
_____ b.	Jamaica	2. Dublin
_____ c.	Italy	3. Jerusalem
_____ d.	Ezra	4. Baghdad
_____ e.	Japan	5. Elihu, Moses and Solomon
_____ f.	1st & 2nd Chronicles	6. Mordecai
_____ g.	Sea of	7. Rome
_____ h.	Israel	8. Unknown
_____ i.	Iraq	9. Tokyo
_____ j.	Ireland	10. Kingston
_____ k.	Job	11. Okhotsk

TRUE OR FALSE — Circle T for true or F for false

T or F   Iraq is also famous for its food, such as sushi, and its origami art.

T or F   The Book of Ezra does not specifically name its author.

T or F   The Dead Sea is also known as The Salt Sea.

T or F   The Book of Nehemiah was written by Job, Elihu, Moses, or Solomon.

T or F   1st Chronicles was written after the exile to help those returning.

T or F   Dublin is the capital of Iceland and is in the continent of Europe.

T or F   1st & 2nd Chronicles are written by Joshua.

T or F   The most popular sport in Jamaica is cricket.

T or F   Israel is the largest producer of fine wine in the world.

T or F   There are six largest oceans in the world.

T or F   Japan is also very rich in petroleum.

LIST THE TOP NINE LARGEST OCEANS AND SEAS

1. _____   2. _____

3. _____   4. _____

5. _____   6. _____

7. _____   8. _____

9. _____

COMPLETE THE FOLLOWING

a. The _____ tower was originally intended for _____ , Spain but the _____ was rejected.

b. There are more _____ words beginning with the _____ 's' than with any other _____ .

c. Japan is known for its _____ art work and for its _____ such as _____ .

d. Italy is _____ or fine _____ , elegance, opera, _____ and architect.

e. Reggae, _____ mento, _____ , and _____ music originated _____ Jamaica.

f. Israel's dairy _____ are the most _____ in the _____ .

g. According to _____ , Iraq is the site of the _____ Garden of _____ .

h. Tea _____ were invented by Thomas _____ . The first _____ were made from _____ .

i. There are no _____ in Ireland and only one _____ (the common _____).

j. The _____ known _____ dates from the Han _____ (221-207 BC), in China.

MEMORIZE AND WRITE

Ezekiel 18:4 _____

_____

_____

Job 23:13 _____

_____

_____

THE LIFE OF DAVID

Recall some of the details of David's life: how he was chosen by God, some of his victories in God, and some of his greatest failures. Write those details out together and discuss how each of you can mimic the qualities that made him "a man after God's own heart," as well as how you can avoid the pitfalls of sin that David fell into.

_____

_____

_____

_____

_____

Bible Word Search

```
S  L  A  I  C  I  F  F  O  B  T  E  O  W  S
D  O  A  B  P  L  S  N  E  E  D  M  O  J  U
B  I  M  B  K  U  X  Y  H  N  J  O  E  T  C
D  S  N  P  E  W  R  P  R  P  O  R  G  A  S
N  R  O  V  G  H  O  I  Y  I  U  R  B  O  A
A  A  N  S  F  R  S  K  A  S  A  S  H  Q  M
H  E  J  Y  P  L  W  H  A  H  A  N  W  T  A
T  L  D  A  W  R  M  L  T  L  T  O  S  K  D
A  I  N  O  R  B  E  H  O  A  K  R  A  G  J
N  T  A  A  T  M  S  M  Z  V  B  C  Y  W  O
M  E  R  A  D  X  X  Y  Q  S  U  O  D  R  N
L  S  M  I  V  E  C  P  R  O  M  I  S  E  A
C  A  P  W  J  N  X  N  S  U  V  J  P  O  D
R  E  I  G  N  H  G  C  U  A  U  L  N  O  A
J  E  J  J  F  C  O  F  D  W  V  H  D  T  B
```

ABSALOM	AMNON	ARK
BATHSHEBA	DAMASCUS	DAVID
GOD	HEBRON	ISRAELITES
JERUSALEM	JONADAB	NATHAN
OFFICIALS	PROMISE	PROPHET
REIGN	SYRIANS	TAMAR
THRONE	URIAH	

Day 8 ~ The Retreat of Absalom

Then Absalom fled...

1) Where did Absalom flee to, and how long did he stay there?_____

_____

_____

2) What instructions did Joab give to the wise woman of Tekoa?_____

_____

3) Describe the appearance of Absalom. _____

_____

Explore God's World

MEMORY VERSES:

Acts 16:31 So they said, "Believe on the Lord Jesus Christ, and you will be saved, you and your household."

Revelation 3:20 "Behold, I stand at the door and knock. If anyone hears My voice and opens the door, I will come in to him and dine with him, and he with Me."

PSALMS

The Psalms have David listed as the author in 73 instances. David's personality and identity are clearly stamped on many of the psalms though he is definitely not the author of the entire collection. Psalms 72 and 127 are attributed to Solomon, David's son and successor. Psalm 90 is a prayer attributed to Moses. Another group of 12 psalms (50 and 73-83) are ascribed to the family of Asaph. The sons of Korah wrote 11 psalms (42, 44-49, 84-85,87-88). Psalm 88 is attributed to Heman, while Psalm 89 is assigned to Ethan the Ezrahite. With the exception of Solomon and Moses, the other authors were priests or Levites who were responsible for providing music for sanctuary worship during David's reign. Fifty of the psalms designate no specific person as author.

PURPOSE

Psalm is the longest book, with 150 individual psalms. It is also one of the most diverse since the psalms deal with such subjects as God and His creation, war, worship, wisdom, sin and evil, judgment, justice, and the coming of the Messiah.

For Your Information

FUN FACTS	THE TOP TEN GRAPE PRODUCING COUNTRIES	JORDAN
1. The word "Buddha" means: awakened one / enlightened one 2. The first typewriter was invented in 1867, by printer and editor Christopher Latham Sholes.	1) Italy 2) France 3) USA 4) Spain 5) China 6) Turkey 7) Iran 8) Argentina 9) Chile 10) Australia	...is in the continent of Asia. Amman is the capital. It is widely believed that Mount Nebo is the burial place of Moses. Jordan is one of the largest producers and exporters of phosphate in the world. Its currency is Jordanian Dinar.

GROUP DISCUSSION AND CLOSING PRAYER

"Patience is not a virtue. It is an achievement."

Vera Nazarian

Day 9 ~ The Conspiracy of Absalom, & David's flight

After this it...

OPENING PRAYER

READ: 2nd Samuel 15:1-12 and 16:1-14

1) Describe how Absalom captivated the hearts of the men of Israel._____
_____
_____

2) What had Ziba brought for David?_____
_____

3) Who was Shimei and how David respond to his curses?_____
_____

Explore God's World

MEMORY VERSES:

Acts 16:31 So they said, "Believe on the Lord Jesus Christ, and you will be saved, you and your household."

Revelation 3:20 "Behold, I stand at the door and knock. If anyone hears My voice and opens the door, I will come in to him and dine with him, and he with Me."

PROVERBS

King Solomon is the principal writer of Proverbs. His name appears in 1:1;10:1; and 25:1. We may also presume Solomon collected and edited proverbs other than his own, for Ecclesiastes 12:9 says, "Not only was the teacher wise, but he also imparted knowledge to the people. He pondered and searched out and set in order many proverbs." Indeed, the Hebrew title Mishle Shelomoh is translated "Proverbs of Solomon".

PURPOSE

Knowledge is nothing more than an accumulation of raw facts, but wisdom is the ability to see people, events, and situations as God sees them. In Proverbs, Solomon reveals the mind of God in matters high and lofty, as well as in ordinary everyday situations. It appears that no topic escaped Solomon's attention. Matters pertaining to personal conduct, sexual relations, business, wealth, charity, ambition, discipline, debt, child-rearing, character, alcohol, politics, revenge, and godliness are among the many topics covered in this rich collection.

For Your Information

FUN FACTS	THE TOP TEN GRAPE PRODUCING COUNTRIES	KAZAKHSTAN
1. In a life time, an average man will shave approximately 20,000 times. 2. According to scientific studies, a rat's performance in a maze can be improved by playing music written by Mozart.	1) Italy 2) France 3) USA 4) Spain 5) China 6) Turkey 7) Iran 8) Argentina 9) Chile 10) Australia	…is in the continent of Asia. Astana is the capital. The biggest landlocked country in the world has a population that is 70% Islam and 26% Christian. Almaty ("rich with apple") is the region where it is thought that the apple originated.

GROUP DISCUSSION AND CLOSING PRAYER

"Do not be discouraged-it may be the last key on the ring that opens the door."

Stansifer

Day 10 ~ The Defeat of Absalom

OPENING PRAYER
READ: 2nd Samuel 17:5-24 and 18:4-18, 33

Then Absalom said...

1) What was David's instructions to Joab, Abishai, and Ittai concerning Absalom?_____
_____
_____

2) How did Absalom get his head caught up in the branches of the oak tree?_____
_____

3) Who killed Absalom, and what were David's final remarks about his son's death?_____
_____

Explore God's World

MEMORY VERSES:
Acts 16:31 So they said, "Believe on the Lord Jesus Christ, and you will be saved, you and your household."

Revelation 3:20 "Behold, I stand at the door and knock. If anyone hears My voice and opens the door, I will come in to him and dine with him, and he with Me."

ECCLESIASTES
The book does not directly identify its author. There are quite a few verses that imply Solomon wrote this book. There are some clues in the context that may suggest a different person authored the book after Solomon's death, possibly several hundred years later. Still, the conventional belief is that the author is indeed Solomon.

PURPOSE
Ecclesiastes is a book of perspective. The narrative of "the Preacher" (KJV), or "the Teacher" (NIV) reveals the depression that inevitably results from seeking happiness in worldly things. This book gives Christians a chance to see the world through the eyes of a person who, though very wise, is trying to find meaning in temporary, human things. Most every form of worldly pleasure is explored by the writer, and none of it gives him any sense of meaning.

For Your Information

FUN FACTS
1. The birth rate in India each year is more than the entire population of Australia.
2. Bruce Lee's movements were so fast that the film actually had to be slowed so one could see them.

THE TOP TEN GRAPE PRODUCING COUNTRIES
1) Italy 2) France 3) USA
4) Spain 5) China 6) Turkey
7) Iran 8) Argentina
9) Chile 10) Australia

KENYA
...is in the continent of Africa. Nairobi is the capital. The "Big Five" animals of Africa are the African lion, the African elephant, the Cape buffalo, the African leopard, and the White/Black rhinoceros. The principal cash crops are tea and coffee. A total of 69 languages are spoken here, but the official languages are Swahili and English.

GROUP DISCUSSION AND CLOSING PRAYER
"Patience is the direct antithesis of anger."
Allan Lokos

Day 11 ~ David's Reinstatement as King

OPENING PRAYER
READ: 2nd Samuel 19:1-18 and 20:1-10

And Joab was told...

1) What did Joab say when David was mourning over Absalom?_____
_____
_____

2) What was David's message to Abiathar and Zadok, the priests?_____
_____

3) Why did Sheba rebel against David and what was the result of it?_____
_____

Explore God's World

MEMORY VERSES:

Acts 16:31 So they said, "Believe on the Lord Jesus Christ, and you will be saved, you and your household."

Revelation 3:20 "Behold, I stand at the door and knock. If anyone hears My voice and opens the door, I will come in to him and dine with him, and he with Me."

SONG OF SOLOMON
Solomon wrote Song of Solomon. This song is one of 1,005 that Solomon wrote (1 Kings 4:32). The title "Song of Songs" is a superlative, meaning "this is the best one."

PURPOSE
This a lyric poem written to extol the virtues of love between a husband and his wife. The poem clearly presents marriage as God's design. A man and woman are to live together within the context of marriage, loving each other spiritually, emotionally, and physically. This book combats two extremes: asceticism (the denial of all pleasure) and hedonism (the pursuit of only pleasure). The marriage profiled in Song of Solomon is a model of care, commitment, and delight.

For Your Information

FUN FACTS
1. In 1812, Henry Bell built a 12 foot steam-powered boat, called "The Comet".
2. Dr. Charles Richard Drew started the idea of a blood bank and a system for the long-term preservation of blood plasma.

THE TOP TEN GRAPE PRODUCING COUNTRIES
1) Italy 2) France 3) USA
4) Spain 5) China 6) Turkey
7) Iran 8) Argentina
9) Chile 10) Australia

KIRIBATI
...is in the continent of Australia (Oceanic). Tarawa Atoll is the capital. Comprised of 33 islands that straddle the equator, Kiribati was once used as a testing ground for nuclear weapons. Coconut, palms and trees are the most common wild plants.

GROUP DISCUSSION AND CLOSING PRAYER

"When I cannot feel the faith of assurance, I live by the fact of God's faithfulness."
Matthew Henry

Day 12 ~ The Psalm of David in Praise to His Lord

OPENING PRAYER
READ: 2nd Samuel 22:1-18

Then David spoke...

1) How did David describe the Lord in verses 2-4?_____
_____
_____

2) How does David describe God's anger in the song?_____
_____

3) How do you define your relationship with the Lord?_____
_____

Explore God's World

MEMORY VERSES:

Acts 16:31 So they said, "Believe on the Lord Jesus Christ, and you will be saved, you and your household."

Revelation 3:20 "Behold, I stand at the door and knock. If anyone hears My voice and opens the door, I will come in to him and dine with him, and he with Me."

ISAIAH
Isaiah 1:1 identifies Isaiah as the author.

PURPOSE
The prophet Isaiah was primarily called to prophesy to the Kingdom of Judah. Judah was going through times of revival and times of rebellion. Judah was threatened with destruction, and promised restoration through the act of repentance from sin and given hopeful expectation of God's deliverance in the future.

For Your Information

FUN FACTS

1. Holding hands with someone you love can alleviate physical pain, as well as stress and fear.

2. The electric iron was invented in 1882 by Henry W. Seeley. His iron weighed almost 15 pounds and took a long time to heat up.

THE TOP TEN GRAPE PRODUCING COUNTRIES

1) Italy 2) France 3) USA
4) Spain 5) China 6) Turkey
7) Iran 8) Argentina
9) Chile 10) Australia

SOUTH KOREA

...is in the continent of Asia. Seoul is the capital. After the US, South Korea is the 2nd largest missionary-sending nation. The country is called the land of Kimchi because of its 187 varieties. Kimchi is a fermented Korean side dish made of vegetables with a variety of seasonings. The martial art of taekwondo originated from here.

GROUP DISCUSSION AND CLOSING PRAYER

"To go through some fires will take great faith, for little faith will fail. We must win the victory in the furnace."

Margaret Bottome

Day 13 ~ David's Last Words

OPENING PRAYER
READ: 2nd Samuel 23:1-7

Then David spoke...

1) What were the last words of David?_____
_____
_____

2) How did David describe evil men?_____
_____

3) What does David say about one who rules in the fear of God?_____
_____

Explore God's World

MEMORY VERSES:

Acts 16:31 So they said, "Believe on the Lord Jesus Christ, and you will be saved, you and your household."

Revelation 3:20 "Behold, I stand at the door and knock. If anyone hears My voice and opens the door, I will come in to him and dine with him, and he with Me."

JEREMIAH
1:1 identifies prophet Jeremiah as the author.

PURPOSE
The book records the final prophecies to Judah, warning of oncoming destruction if the nation does not repent. Jeremiah calls out for the nation to turn back to God. At the same time, he recognizes the inevitability of Judah's destruction, due to its unrepentant idolatry and immorality.

For Your Information

FUN FACTS	THE TOP TEN GRAPE PRODUCING COUNTRIES	NORTH KOREA
1. Your brain is more active when you are sleeping than when you are watching television. 2. Xerography (which means "dry writing" in Greek) is a process of making copies that was invented in 1938 by Chester Floyd Carlson.	1) Italy 2) France 3) USA 4) Spain 5) China 6) Turkey 7) Iran 8) Argentina 9) Chile 10) Australia	...is in the continent of Asia. Pyongyang is the capital. Human rights organizations accuse North Korea of having one of the worst human rights records of any nation. The country has the 4th largest army and largest submarine fleet in the world. The country's religion is the worship of the Supreme Leader.

GROUP DISCUSSION AND CLOSING PRAYER

"Sometimes I wonder if I have learned anything except at the end of God's rod. When my classroom is darkest, I see best."

Charles H. Spurgeon

Day 14 ~ Week in Review

MEMORIZE AND WRITE

Acts 16:31 _____

_____

_____

Revelation 3:20_____

_____

_____

TRUE OR FALSE — Circle T for true or F for false

T or F   Kazakhstan is the biggest landlocked country in the world.

T or F   Kenya's official languages are Swahili and English.

T or F   The Book of Isaiah was written by the prophet Isaiah.

T or F   North Korea is called the land of Kimchi because of its with 187 varieties.

T or F   Jeremiah calls out for the nation to turn back to God.

T or F   Psalms the longest book in the Bible, with 160 individual psalms.

T or F   Italy, France and USA are the three largest grape producing countries.

T or F   Patience is the direct antithesis of anger.

T or F   Kenya's currency is the Kenyan Dinar.

T or F   Kazakhstan was once used as a testing ground for nuclear weapons.

T or F   Korea, South has the 4th-largest army and submarine fleet in the world.

LIST THE TOP TEN GRAPE PRODUCING COUNTRIES

1. _____   2. _____

3. _____   4. _____

5. _____   6. _____

7. _____   8. _____

9. _____   10. _____

COMPLETE THE FOLLOWING

a. The _____ rate in India each _____ is more than the entire _____ of Australia.

b. The first _____ was invented in _____ by printer and editor _____ Latham _____.

c. The principal _____ crops of Kenya are _____ and _____.

d. In a life time, an _____ man will _____ approximately _____ times.

e. Kiribati was once _____ as a _____ ground for nuclear _____.

f. Jordan is one of the _____ producers and _____ of _____ in the world.

g. _____ Korea has the 4th _____ army and the largest _____ fleet in the _____.

h. After the _____, South Korea is the _____ largest _____-sending nation.

i. The Hebrew title "Mishle" _____ is translated "_____ of Solomon."

j. Almaty ("rich with _____") is the _____ where it is _____ that the apple _____.

j. Your brain is more _____ when you are _____ than when you are _____ television.

MATCH THE FOLLOWING

_____ a. Kenya	1. David
_____ b. Jeremiah	2. Seoul
_____ c. Isaiah	3. Amman
_____ d. South Korea	4. Nairobi
_____ e. Psalms	5. Prophet Jeremiah
_____ f. Kazakhstan	6. Tarawa Atoll
_____ g. Song of Solomon	7. Astana
_____ h. North Korea	8. Prophet Isaiah
_____ i. Kiribati	9. King Solomon
_____ j. Jordon	10. Pyongyang

THE EXAMPLE OF DAVID

What can you learn from David when it comes to how we should praise the Lord in our lives? How can you live your worship to the Lord?

_____

_____

_____

_____

Best Friends David & Johnathan Coloring Activity

Note, you may make copies of this page to color if multiple family members in the same household want to color the illustration.

Day 15 ~ The Decline of David & the Exaltation of Solomon

OPENING PRAYER

READ: 1st Kings 1:1-4, 28-53; 2:1-4, and 10-12

Now King David...

1) Why was Abishag brought before the King?_____
_____
_____

2) Who was Adonijah, and what did he desire?_____
_____

3) What instructions did David give to Solomon before his death?_____
_____

Explore God's World

MEMORY VERSES:

Jeremiah 31:3 he Lord has appeared of old to me, saying: "Yes, I have loved you with an everlasting love; Therefore with loving kindness I have drawn you."

Isaiah 6:8 Also I heard the voice of the Lord, saying: "Whom shall I send, And who will go for Us?" Then I said, "Here am I! Send me."

LAMENTATIONS

The book does not explicitly identify its author. The tradition is that the Jeremiah wrote Lamentations. This view is highly likely considering the author was a witness of the Babylonians destroying Jerusalem. 2nd Chronicles 35:25; 36:21-22

PURPOSE

As a result of Judah's continued and unrepentant idolatry, God allowed the Babylonians to besiege, plunder, burn, and destroy the city of Jerusalem. Solomon's Temple, which had stood for approximately 400 years, was burned to the ground. Jeremiah, an eyewitness to these events, wrote Lamentations as a lament for what occurred to Judah and Jerusalem.

For Your Information

FUN FACTS	THE TOP TEN COUNTRIES WITH THE LARGEST MUSLIM POPULATION	KOSOVO
1. It takes an interaction of 72 muscles to produce audible human speech. 2. The telephone (meaning "far sound") is the most widely used telecommunications device. It was invented in 1876 by Alexander Graham Bell (with Thomas Watson).	1) Indonesia 2) India 3) Pakistan 4) Bangladesh 5) Nigeria 6) Egypt 7) Iran 8) Turkey 9) Algeria 10) Morocco	...is in the continent of Europe; Pristina is the capital. Kosovo is the newest nation of the 21st century. Nineteen countries maintain embassies here; as of 11 February 2014, 108 countries recognize the Republic. Albanian and Serbian are the official languages.

GROUP DISCUSSION AND CLOSING PRAYER

"Faith, when walking through the dark with God, only asks Him to hold His hand more tightly."

Phillips Brooks

Day 16 ~ The Establishment of the Solomonic Kingdom

Now Adonijah the son...

OPENING PRAYER

READ: 1st Kings 2:13-24, 26-31, and 36-46

1) What was Adonijah's request to Bathsheba?_____
_____
_____

2) Why did Solomon put Joab to death?_____
_____

3) What was Solomon's command to Shimei?_____
_____

Explore God's World

MEMORY VERSES:

Jeremiah 31:3 he Lord has appeared of old to me, saying: "Yes, I have loved you with an everlasting love; Therefore with loving kindness I have drawn you."

Isaiah 6:8 Also I heard the voice of the Lord, saying: "Whom shall I send, And who will go for Us?" Then I said, "Here am I! Send me."

EZEKIEL

1:3 identifies Ezekiel as the author. He was a contemporary of both Jeremiah and Daniel.

PURPOSE

He ministered to his generation, who were both exceedingly sinful and thoroughly hopeless. By means of his prophetic ministry, he attempted to bring them to immediate repentance and to confidence in the distant future.

He taught that:

(1) God works through human messengers
(2) Even in defeat and despair God's people need to affirm God's sovereignty
(3) God's Word never fails
(4) God is present and can be worshiped anywhere
(5) People must obey God if they expect to receive blessings
(6) God's Kingdom will come.

For Your Information

FUN FACTS	THE TOP TEN COUNTRIES WITH THE LARGEST MUSLIM POPULATION	KUWAIT
1. The windshield wiper was invented by Mary Anderson in 1903. 2. Mosquito has 47 teeth and there are more than 3,500 species of mosquitoes.	1) Indonesia 2) India 3) Pakistan 4) Bangladesh 5) Nigeria 6) Egypt 7) Iran 8) Turkey 9) Algeria 10) Morocco	...is in the continent of Asia; Kuwait City is the capital. Comprised of 9 islands, Kuwait has the world's 5th largest oil reserves and is the 8th richest country in the world. Yet, it's one of the smallest countries in the world in terms of land area. Soccer is the national sports of Kuwait.

GROUP DISCUSSION AND CLOSING PRAYER

"Obedience is a fruit of faith, patience is the early blossom on the tree of faith."

Christina Rossetti

Day 17 ~ The Great Wisdom of Solomon

OPENING PRAYER
READ: 1st Kings 3:10-28; and 4:26-34

The speech pleased...

1) For what did Solomon ask the Lord?_____
_____
_____

2) What case did the two women bring unto the king?_____
_____

3) Describe in few words Solomon's wealth and wisdom. _____
_____

Explore God's World

MEMORY VERSES:

Jeremiah 31:3 he Lord has appeared of old to me, saying: "Yes, I have loved you with an everlasting love; Therefore with loving kindness I have drawn you."

Isaiah 6:8 Also I heard the voice of the Lord, saying: "Whom shall I send, And who will go for Us?" Then I said, "Here am I! Send me."

DANIEL
9:2 and 10:2 states its author. Jesus mentions Daniel the author as well Matthew 24:15.
PURPOSE
In 605 B.C., Nebuchadnezzar, King of Babylon, had conquered Judah and deported many of its inhabitants to Babylon, including Daniel. He served in the royal court of Nebuchadnezzar and several rulers who followed him. The Book records the actions, prophecies, and visions of Daniel.

For Your Information

FUN FACTS	THE TOP TEN COUNTRIES WITH THE LARGEST MUSLIM POPULATION	KYRGYZSTAN
1. Two-thirds of the people on earth have never seen snow. 2. The history of glassmaking can be traced back to 3500 BC in Mesopotamia. 3. The first method of refrigeration (cooling air by the evaporation of liquids in a vacuum) was invented in1748 by William Cullen of the University of Glasgow, Scotland.	1) Indonesia 2) India 3) Pakistan 4) Bangladesh 5) Nigeria 6) Egypt 7) Iran 8) Turkey 9) Algeria 10) Morocco	…is in the continent of Asia; Bishkek is the capital. Kyrgyz is derived from the Turkic word means forty, ("We are forty") This is a landlocked and mountainous country with the world's largest walnut trees. Kyrgyzstan is bordered by Kazakhstan to the north, Uzbekistan to the west, Tajikistan to the southwest, and China to the east.

GROUP DISCUSSION AND CLOSING PRAYER
"It wasn't raining when Noah built the ark."
Howard Ruff

Helping Parents Develop Their Children's Love for God and for People

21

Day 18 ~ The Building Program of Solomon's Temple

OPENING PRAYER
READ: 1st Kings 5:1-12; 6:1,11-14, and 37-38

Now Hiram king...

1) How many men did Solomon need to construct the temple?_____

_____

_____

2) When did the building of the temple begin, and when was it completed?_____

_____

3) What promise did God make with Solomon in verses 11-13?_____

_____

Explore God's World

MEMORY VERSES:

Jeremiah 31:3 he Lord has appeared of old to me, saying: "Yes, I have loved you with an everlasting love; Therefore with loving kindness I have drawn you."

Isaiah 6:8 Also I heard the voice of the Lord, saying: "Whom shall I send, And who will go for Us?" Then I said, "Here am I! Send me."

HOSEA

1:1 identifies Hosea as the author. It is Hosea's personal account of his prophetic messages to the children of God and to the world. Hosea is the only prophet of Israel who left any written prophecies which were recorded during the later years of his life.

PURPOSE

Hosea wrote to remind the Israelites, and us, that ours is a loving God whose loyalty to His covenant people is unwavering. In spite of Israel's continual turning to false gods, God's steadfast love is portrayed as the long-suffering husband of the unfaithful wife. His message is also one of warning to those who would turn their backs on God's love. Through the symbolic presentation of the marriage of Hosea and Gomer, God's love for the idolatrous nation of Israel is displayed in a rich metaphor in the themes of sin, judgment, forgiveness, and love.

For Your Information

FUN FACTS	THE TOP TEN COUNTRIES WITH THE LARGEST MUSLIM POPULATION	LAOS
1. A humming bird weighs less than a penny. 2. Hammerhead sharks are born with soft heads so they won't jam their mother's birth canal. 3. Overly aggressive and overly permissive parents are equally likely to have children who bully.	1) Indonesia 2) India 3) Pakistan 4) Bangladesh 5) Nigeria 6) Egypt 7) Iran 8) Turkey 9) Algeria 10) Morocco	...is in the continent of Asia. Vientiane is the capital. The official tourism slogan is "Simply Beautiful." Lao is the written language while Thai and Hmong are spoken ones. The country is an increasingly suffering from environmental problems, which is made worse by deforestation.

GROUP DISCUSSION AND CLOSING PRAYER

"Wisdom is knowing what to do with what you know."

Chuck Smith

Day 19 ~ The Building Program of Solomon's Kingdom

Now King Solomon...

OPENING PRAYER

READ: 1st Kings 7:13-23; 8:4-21, and 62-66

1) Who did all the bronze work for Solomon's buildings?_____

_____

_____

2) Explain what the Ark of the Covenant represents._____

_____

3) How many bulls and sheep did Solomon offer to the Lord?_____

_____

Explore God's World

MEMORY VERSES:

Jeremiah 31:3
The Lord has appeared of old to me, saying: "Yes, I have loved you with an everlasting love; Therefore with loving kindness I have drawn you."

Isaiah 6:8 Also I heard the voice of the Lord, saying: "Whom shall I send, And who will go for Us?" Then I said, "Here am I! Send me."

JOEL
Verse 1 identifies Joel as the author.

PURPOSE
Judah, the setting for the book, is devastated by a vast horde of locusts. Destroying everything - the fields of grain, the vineyards, the gardens, and the trees. Joel symbolically describes the locusts as a marching human army and views all of this as divine judgment coming against the nation for her sins. The book is highlighted by two major events. One is the invasion of locusts and the other the outpouring of the Spirit. The initial fulfillment of this is quoted by Peter in Acts 2 as having taken place at Pentecost.

For Your Information

FUN FACTS	THE TOP TEN COUNTRIES WITH THE LARGEST MUSLIM POPULATION	LATVIA
1. Every 90 seconds, one woman dies from a pregnancy or childbirth complication. 2. During pregnancy, some pregnant women crave nonfood items, such as paper, clay, and chalk, etc. This eating disorder is called "Pica."	1) Indonesia 2) India 3) Pakistan 4) Bangladesh 5) Nigeria 6) Egypt 7) Iran 8) Turkey 9) Algeria 10) Morocco	…is in the continent of Europe; Riga is the capital. In the late 12th century, the Pope Celestine III sent the first missionaries there seeking converts. There are 2,256 lakes that are bigger than 2.5 acres and over 12,500 rivers. Euro is the currency.

GROUP DISCUSSION AND CLOSING PRAYER

"Yet, God's plans for you, and His way of bringing about His plans are infinitely wise."

Madame Guyon

Day 20 ~ The Events of Solomon's Reign

OPENING PRAYER
READ: 1st Kings 9:1-9; 10:1-13; 11:1-12, and 41-43

And it came to...

1) What was the promise the Lord made with King Solomon?_____
_____

2) What gifts did the Queen of Sheba bring for King Solomon?_____
_____

3) Why was the Lord not pleased with King Solomon?_____
_____
_____

Explore God's World

MEMORY VERSES:

Jeremiah 31:3 he Lord has appeared of old to me, saying: "Yes, I have loved you with an everlasting love; Therefore with loving kindness I have drawn you."

Isaiah 6:8 Also I heard the voice of the Lord, saying: "Whom shall I send, And who will go for Us?" Then I said, "Here am I! Send me."

AMOS
Verse 1 identifies the author as Amos.

PURPOSE
God calls him, even though he lacks an education or a priestly background. Amos' mission was to his neighbor to the north, Israel. His messages of impending doom and captivity for the nation, because of her sins, are largely unpopular and unheeded. However, because not since the days of Solomon have times been so good in Israel. Amos' ministry takes place while Jeroboam II reigns over Israel, and Uzziah reigns over Judah.

For Your Information

FUN FACTS	THE TOP TEN COUNTRIES WITH THE LARGEST MUSLIM POPULATION	LEBANON
1. M&Ms were invented in 1941 for soldiers to enjoy chocolate without the candy melting. 2. The largest natural bridge on Earth was virtually unknown to the rest of the world until it was observed on Google Earth. It is called the "Fairy bridge". It is located in China.	1) Indonesia 2) India 3) Pakistan 4) Bangladesh 5) Nigeria 6) Egypt 7) Iran 8) Turkey 9) Algeria 10) Morocco	...is in the continent of Asia; Beirut is the capital. The native cedar tree of Lebanon is mentioned 75 times in the O.T. The country has 17 official religions with their own family law and religious courts. 59.7% are Muslim, while 39% are Christian, and 1.3% is of other religions. Basketball is one of the most popular sports in Lebanon.

GROUP DISCUSSION AND CLOSING PRAYER

"When you have faith, you need not retreat. You can stop the Enemy wherever you encounter him."

Marshal Ferdina

Day 21 ~ Week in Review

MATCH THE FOLLOWING

_____ a. Laos

_____ b. Kuwait

_____ c. Joel

_____ d. Daniel

_____ e. Lamentations

_____ f. Ezekiel

_____ g. Lebanon

_____ h. Amos

_____ i. Kyrgyzstan

_____ j. Kosovo

_____ k. Hosea

_____ l. Latvia

1. Bishkek
2. Prophet Ezekiel
3. Pristina
4. Riga
5. Jeremiah
6. Joel
7. Prophet Hosea
8. Daniel
9. Kuwait City
10. Vientiane
11. Unknown
12. Beirut

TRUE OR FALSE — Circle T for true or F for false

T or F   Kyrgyz is derived from the Turkic word means twenty "We are twenty."

T or F   Daniel records the actions, prophecies, and visions of the prophet Daniel.

T or F   Laos is increasingly suffering from environmental problems with floods.

T or F   The official languages of Kosovo are Albanian and Serbian.

T or F   The native cedar tree of Lebanon is mentioned 175 times in the Old Testament.

T or F   The Pope sent the 1st missionaries to Latvia in 16th century.

T or F   Solomon's Temple, which had stood for 400 years, was burned to the ground.

T or F   Ezekiel ministered to those who were both exceedingly sinful and thoroughly hopeless.

T or F   Judah, the setting of Joel, is devastated by a vast horde of flies.

T or F Amos is a stone builder and a fruit picker from the Judean village of Tekoa.

LIST THE TOP TEN COUNTRIES WITH THE LARGEST MUSLIM POPULATION

1. _____   2. _____

3. _____   4. _____

5. _____   6. _____

7. _____   8. _____

9. _____   10. _____

COMPLETE THE FOLLOWING

a. The official _____ slogan of Laos is "Simply_____."

b. Kuwait has the _____ 5th _____ largest oil ____ and is the 8th country in the _____.

c. In Lebanon _____ are Muslim while 39% are_____, and 1.3% is of other_____.

d. Albanian and _____ are the official _____ of_____.

e. In Latvia there are _____ lakes that are _____ than _____ acres and over_____ rivers.

f. The _____ of glassmaking can be_____ back to 3500 BC in_____.

g. It takes an _____ of 72 muscles to _____ audible human_____.

h. The windshield wiper was _____ by Mary_____ in_____.

i. Kyrgyzstan is_____ and mountainous and has the world's _____ trees of _____ fruit.

MEMORIZE AND WRITE

Jeremiah 31:3_____

_____

_____

Isaiah 6:8_____

_____

_____

THE WISDOM OF SOLOMON

Describe Solomon's wealth and wisdom, and share why God blessed Solomon with so much more than just the wisdom Solomon requested.

_____

_____

_____

_____

_____

_____

_____

_____

The Original Tabernacle Coloring Activity

Note, you may make copies of this page to color if multiple family members in the same household want to color the illustration.

Day 22 ~ Elijah & the Drought

OPENING PRAYER
READ: 1st Kings 17:1-24

Then the word of...

1) Who was Elijah, and from where did he get his food? _____
_____
_____

2) After the land dried up, where did God send Elijah for food? _____
_____

3) What was the first miracle performed at the widow's house? _____
_____

Explore God's World

MEMORY VERSES:

John 1:12-13 "But as many as received Him, to them He gave the right to become children of God, to those who believe in His name: who were born, not of blood, nor of the will of the flesh, nor of the will of man, but of God."

OBADIAH
Verse 1 identifies the author as Obadiah.

PURPOSE
The shortest book in the Old Testament, is only 21 verses long. He is a prophet of God, whom God uses to condemn Edom for sins against both God and Israel. The Edomites are descendants of Esau and the Israelites are descendants of his twin brother, Jacob. A quarrel between the brothers has affected their descendants for over 1,000 years. This division caused the Edomites to forbid Israel to cross their land during the Israelites' Exodus from Egypt. Edom's sins of pride now required a strong word of judgment from the Lord.

For Your Information

FUN FACTS	SEVEN COUNTRIES WITH THE LARGEST ARMIES	LESOTHO
1. Scrabble, the word game, was developed by Alfred Mosher Butts in 1948. 2. The first practical electric light bulb was made in 1878 simultaneously (and independently) by Joseph Wilson Swan and Thomas Alva Edison.	1. People's Republic of China: 2,285,000 2. United States of America: 1,429,995 3. India: 1,325,000 4. Democratic People's Republic of Korea: 1,106,000 5. Russian Federation: 1,040,000 6. Republic of Korea: 687,000 7. Turkey: 664,060	…is in the continent of Africa. Maseru is the capital. The name Lesotho translates roughly into "the land of the people who speak Sotho". About 40% of the population lives below the international poverty line, at about $1.25 (USA) a day.

GROUP DISCUSSION AND CLOSING PRAYER

"God may not give us an easy journey to the promised land, but He will give us a safe one."

Horatius Bonar

Day 23 ~ Elijah & King Ahab

The Elijah Said...

1) Why did King Ahab say to Elijah, "Is that you, Oh troubler of Israel"? _____
_____
_____

2) What happened when the prophets of Baal called on their god? _____
_____

3) What did Elijah say to King Ahab, and how did the drought end? _____
_____

Explore God's World

MEMORY VERSES:

John 1:12-13 "But as many as received Him, to them He gave the right to become children of God, to those who believe in His name: who were born, not of blood, nor of the will of the flesh, nor of the will of man, but of God."

JONAH
Verse 1 specifically identifies the author as Jonah.
PURPOSE
Disobedience and revival are the key themes in this book. Jonah's experience in the belly of the fish provides him with an opportunity to seek a unique deliverance, as he repents. His initial disobedience leads not only to his personal revival, but to that of the Ninevites, as well. Many classify the revival, which Jonah brings to Nineveh, as one of the greatest in history.

For Your Information

FUN FACTS	SEVEN COUNTRIES WITH THE LARGEST ARMIES	LIBERIA
1. The first working airplane was invented, designed, built, and flown by the Wright brothers. 2. The paper clip was invented in 1890 or 1899 by Johann Vaaler. His original paper clip was a thin spring-steel wire with triangular or square ends and two "tongues."	1. People's Republic of China: 2,285,000 2. United States of America: 1,429,995 3. India: 1,325,000 4. Democratic People's Republic of Korea: 1,106,000 5. Russian Federation: 1,040,000 6. Republic of Korea: 687,000 7. Turkey: 664,060	...is in the continent of Africa. Monrovia is the capital. The country is literally a bird-haven, with more than 700 bird species, including the bee warbler - a bird that is a bit larger than a honey bee. Liberia means "Land of the Free" in Latin. It was founded in 1822 by freed American and Caribbean slaves, and is Africa's oldest republic.

GROUP DISCUSSION AND CLOSING PRAYER

"Remember, the goal is simply to carry the cargo and make it to port."

Maltbie D. Babcock

Day 24 ~ Elijah's Flight to Horeb

And Lot also...

OPENING PRAYER
READ: 1st Kings 19:1-21

1) Who threatened Elijah's life?_____

_____

2) What did God provide Elijah to eat in the wilderness?_____

_____

3) Who was Elisha, and why did he become Elijah's servant?_____

_____

Explore God's World

John 1:12-13 "But as many as received Him, to them He gave the right to become children of God, to those who believe in His name: who were born, not of blood, nor of the will of the flesh, nor of the will of man, but of God."

MICAH
Verse 1 identifies the author as Micah.

PURPOSE
The message is a complex mixture of judgment and hope. On the one hand, the prophecies announce judgment upon Israel for social evils, corrupt leadership and idolatry. This judgment was expected to culminate in the destruction of both Samaria and Jerusalem. On the other hand, the book proclaims not merely the restoration of the nation, but the transformation and exaltation of Israel and Jerusalem. The messages of hope and doom are not necessarily contradictory, because restoration and transformation take place only after judgment.

For Your Information

FUN FACTS	SEVEN COUNTRIES WITH THE LARGEST ARMIES	LIBYA
1. There is enough iron in a non-malnourished human body to make a nail. 2. Scissors were invented in ancient Egypt thousands of years ago. (1500 B.C.) Modern cross-bladed scissors were invented in ancient Rome. (100 A.D.)	1. People's Republic of China: 2,285,000 2. United States of America: 1,429,995 3. India: 1,325,000 4. Democratic People's Republic of Korea: 1,106,000 5. Russian Federation: 1,040,000 6. Republic of Korea: 687,000 7. Turkey: 664,060	...is in the continent of Africa. Tripoli is the capital. All its citizens are provided with free education. The government provides free houses or apartments to all newly-married couples. Libya holds the largest proven oil reserves in Africa.

GROUP DISCUSSION AND CLOSING PRAYER

"My prayer today is that God would make me an extraordinary Christian."

George Whitefield

Day 25 ~ A Prophetic's Condemnation of Ahab

Suddenly a prophet...

OPENING PRAYER
READ: 1st Kings 20:13-40

1) Why did God become angry with Ahab?_____

_____

2) How did God answer Ben-Hadad's challenge?_____

_____

3) Why was the man killed by the lion?_____

_____

Explore God's World

MEMORY VERSES:

John 1:12-13 "But as many as received Him, to them He gave the right to become children of God, to those who believe in His name: who were born, not of blood, nor of the will of the flesh, nor of the will of man, but of God."

NAHUM

The author Identifies himself as Nahum (in the Hebrew "Consoler" or "Comforter") the Elkoshite (1:1). There are many theories as to where that city was, though there is no conclusive evidence. One such theory is that it refers to the city later called Capernaum (which literally means "the village of Nahum") at the Sea of Galilee.

PURPOSE

Nahum did not write as a warning or "call to repentance" for the people of Nineveh. God had already sent them Jonah 150 years earlier with His promise of what would happen if they continued in their evil ways. The people at that time had repented, but now lived just as badly, if not worse, than they did before. The Assyrians had become absolutely brutal in their conquest (hanging the bodies of their victims on poles and putting their skin on the walls of their tents among other atrocities). Now he was telling the people of Judah to not despair because God had pronounced judgment, and the Assyrians would soon be getting just what they deserved.

For Your Information

FUN FACTS	SEVEN COUNTRIES WITH THE LARGEST ARMIES	LITHUANIA
1. In Switzerland, it is illegal to own only one guinea pig, because they are prone to loneliness. 2. The San Francisco cable cars are the only mobile National Monument in the world.	1. People's Republic of China: 2,285,000 2. United States of America: 1,429,995 3. India: 1,325,000 4. Democratic People's Republic of Korea: 1,106,000 5. Russian Federation: 1,040,000 6. Republic of Korea: 687,000 7. Turkey: 664,060	...is in the continent of Europe; Vilnius is the capital. In 1387, the first documented school was established at Vilnius Cathedral. The country was historically home to a significant Jewish community. Lithuania has diplomatic relations with 149 countries.

GROUP DISCUSSION AND CLOSING PRAYER

"Great faith is exhibited not so much in doing, as in suffering."

Charles Parkhurst

Day 26 ~ Elijah's Condemnation of Ahab

OPENING PRAYER
READ: 1st Kings 21:1-29

And it came to...

1) What did Ahab want from Naboth?_____
_____
_____

2) How did Jezebel plot to kill Naboth?_____
_____

3) What was God's judgment against Ahab for Naboth's murder?_____
_____

Explore God's World

MEMORY VERSES:

John 1:12-13 "But as many as received Him, to them He gave the right to become children of God, to those who believe in His name: who were born, not of blood, nor of the will of the flesh, nor of the will of man, but of God."

HABAKKUK
1:1 identifies the Book as an vision from Habakkuk.
PURPOSE
Habakkuk wondered why God allowed His chosen people to go through the current suffering at the hands of their enemies. God answered, and Habakkuk's faith was restored.

For Your Information

FUN FACTS	SEVEN COUNTRIES WITH THE LARGEST ARMIES	LIECHTENSTEIN
1. X-rays were discovered in 1895 by Wilhelm K. Roentgen. He described this new form of radiation that allowed him to photograph objects that were hidden behind opaque shields. 2. The first rubber band was made in 1845 by Stephen Perry of the rubber manufacturing company Messers Perry and Co.UK. The bands were to hold papers or envelopes together.	1. People's Republic of China: 2,285,000 2. United States of America: 1,429,995 3. India: 1,325,000 4. Democratic People's Republic of Korea: 1,106,000 5. Russian Federation: 1,040,000 6. Republic of Korea: 687,000 7. Turkey: 664,060	...is in the continent of Europe. Vaduz is the capital. Famous for its private banks. Though Liechtenstein is the smallest country, it is the richest (by measure of GDP per capita). The official language is German. Most citizens speak an Alemannic dialect of German that is highly divergent from Standard German.

GROUP DISCUSSION AND CLOSING PRAYER

"Prayer is a wonderful thing, and each person of the Trinity is involved in every acceptable prayer."

J. Angell James

Day 27 ~ The Lord's Judgment on Ahaziah

OPENING PRAYER
READ: 2nd Kings 1:1-18

Then Elisha said...

1) Where did Ahaziah send his messengers to inquire whether he would recover or not?_____
_____
_____

2) What happened to those fifty men who came to capture Elijah?_____
_____

3) What words were spoken for Ahaziah by Elijah?_____
_____

Explore God's World

MEMORY VERSES:

John 1:12-13 "But as many as received Him, to them He gave the right to become children of God, to those who believe in His name: who were born, not of blood, nor of the will of the flesh, nor of the will of man, but of God."

ZEPHANIAH
Verse 1 identifies the author as Zephaniah. The name Zephaniah means "defended by God."

PURPOSE
This is a message of judgment and encouragement that contains three major doctrines:
1) God is sovereign over all nations.
2) The wicked will be punished, and the righteous will be vindicated on the day of judgment.
3) God blesses those who repent and trust in Him.

For Your Information

FUN FACTS	SEVEN COUNTRIES WITH THE LARGEST ARMIES	LUXEMBOURG
1. Human fingernails can grow up to four times faster than toenails. 2. Joseph and Jacques Etienne Montgolfier were two French brothers who made the first successful hot-air balloon. Their first balloon was launched in December,1782.	1. People's Republic of China: 2,285,000 2. United States of America: 1,429,995 3. India: 1,325,000 4. Democratic People's Republic of Korea: 1,106,000 5. Russian Federation: 1,040,000 6. Republic of Korea: 687,000 7. Turkey: 664,060	...is in the continent of Europe. Luxembourg is the capital. The country is best known for its wine region, and its historic sites, like the Military Museum, the Vianden Castle, and the American Military Cemetery. Luxembourg has the only university in the country.

GROUP DISCUSSION AND CLOSING PRAYER

"I will have reached the point of greatest strength once I have learned to wait for hope."

George Matheson

Day 28 ~ Week in Review

MEMORIZE AND WRITE

John 1:12-13_____

_____

_____

TRUE OR FALSE — Circle T for true or F for false

T or F   Liberia means "Land of the Free" in Latin.

T or F   Libya provides all its citizens with free education.

T or F   The author of the Book of Micah is unknown.

T or F   Lesotho is rich in natural resources and hi-technology

T or F   Liechtenstein is famous for its state run banks.

T or F   The first documented school was established in 1387 at Vilnius Cathedral.

T or F   Luxembourg has the only university in the country.

T or F   Obadiah, the shortest book in the Old Testament, is only 39 verses long.

T or F   The name Zephaniah means "defended by God."

T or F   Disobedience and revival are the key themes in Jonah.

LIST SEVEN COUNTRIES WITH THE WORLD'S LARGEST ARMIES

1. _____ 2. _____

3. _____ 4. _____

5. _____ 6. _____

7. _____

COMPLETE THE FOLLOWING

a. Liechtenstein is the_____nation yet the_____(by measure of_____per capita)

b. The_____of the Book of Micah is a _____mixture of_____and_____.

c. The word_____Scrabble was_____by Alfred Mosher_____in 1948.

d. Lithuania was_____home to a significant _____ community.

e. The name Lesotho_____roughly into "the_____of the people who speak_____".

f. Luxembourg is_____known for its_____region, and historic_____, like their Military
Museum, the_____Castle, and the American_____Cemetery.

g. Liberia is literally a_____-_____with its 700 bird_____.

h. _____and_____are the key_____in the_____of Jonah.

i. Libya's_____provides free_____or apartments to all newly-_____couples.

MATCH THE FOLLOWING

_____ a. Libya	1. Luxembourg
_____ b. China	2. Monrovia
_____ c. Liechtenstein	3. 1,325,000
_____ d. Luxembourg	4. Vaduz
_____ e. Lesotho	5. Skopje
_____ f. Liberia	6. Vilnius
_____ g. India	7. 2,285,000
_____ h. Lithuania	8. Maseru
_____ i. Macedonia	9. Tripoli

THE PROPHET ELIJAH

List at least three miracles of divine protection that God provided for Elijah, and describe at least three different times God used Elijah to deliver God's messages to people.

_____

_____

_____

_____

_____

_____

_____

_____

_____

_____

_____

Bible Word Search

```
J E Z C G H T T L U X S K O L
J L J N N N N H H I Y N V M E
R I Y X E A I N R G O J X T B
G S E B V L A K R E U N L U E
V H T R J B I E P S A O Y Q Z
J A E Y O S X J R N N T R W E
U S Q T B S W E A A W J E D J
D I H Y L E G M Y H Z Z N N J
G F O O D N I A T E H P O R P
M D N L E R V W W D L F Z R H
E M Z S A E P R O V I S I O N
N V S C U D A H A Z I A H B L
T E L G A L T D W O D I W A H
M E B N O I D L S V U F A H G
X S G G Z W S X J M Q B X A K
```

AHAB	AHAZIAH	BAAL
DROUGHT	ELIJAH	ELISHA
FOOD	JEZEBEL	JUDGMENT
KING	LION	MESSENGERS
MIRACLE	NABOTH	PROPHET
PROVISION	SERVANT	THREATEN
WIDOW	WILDERNESS	

Day 29 ~ The Transition from Elijah to Elisha

OPENING PRAYER
READ: 2nd Kings 2:1-25

And it came to...

1) How was Elijah taken into heaven?_____
_____
_____

2) Elisha requested what from Elijah?_____
_____

3) What was the first miracle Elisha performed?_____
_____

Explore God's World

MEMORY VERSES:

Exodus 34:7 "Keeping loyal love for thousands, forgiving iniquity, and transgression, and sin. But He by no means leaves the guilty unpunished, responding to the transgression of fathers by dealing with children and children's children, to the third and fourth generation."

HAGGAI
Verse 1 identifies the author as Haggai.

PURPOSE
Haggai sought to challenge the people of God concerning their priorities. He called them to reverence and glorify God by building the Temple, in spite of local and official opposition. Haggai admonished them to not be discouraged because this Temple would not be quite as richly decorated as Solomon's. He exhorted them to turn from the uncleanness of their ways and to trust in God's sovereign power. The Book is a reminder of the problems the people of God faced at this time, how the people courageously trusted in God and how God provided for their needs.

For Your Information

FUN FACTS

1. Zacharias Janssen was a lensmaker who invented the first compound microscope in 1595.

2. Gunpowder was invented in China, probably during the 1000's. It is composed with 75% saltpeter or potassium nitrate, 15% powdered charcoal, and 10% sulphur.

SEVEN RISKIEST CITIES PRONE TO EARTHQUAKES, HURRICANES, CYCLONES AND TSUNAMIS

1) Tokyo-Yokohama, Japan
2) Manila, Philippines
3) Pearl River Delta, China
4) Osaka-Kobe, Japan
5) Jakarta, Indonesia
6) Nagoya, Japan
7) Kolkata, India

MACEDONIA

...is in the continent of Europe. Skopje is the capital. This is the only country that gained independence from Yugoslavia without any bloodshed. Orthodox Christianity is the major faith making up 64.7% of the population.

GROUP DISCUSSION AND CLOSING PRAYER

"Give all He asks, and take all He promises."

Samuel Dickey Gordon

Day 30 ~ Elisha's Ministry

OPENING PRAYER
READ: 2nd Kings 3:1-27

Now Jehoram the...

1) Who became king of Israel after Ahaziah died? _____
_____

2) What was the conversation between Elisha and the king of Israel? _____
_____

3) What did the Moabites see when the sun was shining on the water? _____
_____
_____

Explore God's World

MEMORY VERSES:

Exodus 34:7 "Keeping loyal love for thousands, forgiving iniquity, and transgression, and sin. But He by no means leaves the guilty unpunished, responding to the transgression of fathers by dealing with children and children's children, to the third and fourth generation."

ZECHARIAH
Verse 1 identifies the author as Zechariah.

PURPOSE
Zechariah emphasized that God has used His prophets to teach, warn, and correct His people. Unfortunately, they refused to listen. Their sin brought God's punishment. The book also bears evidence that even prophecy could be corrupted. History shows that in this period prophecy fell into disfavor among the Jews, leading to the period between the Testaments when no lasting prophetic voice spoke to God's people.

For Your Information

FUN FACTS	SEVEN RISKIEST CITIES PRONE TO EARTHQUAKES, HURRICANES, CYCLONES AND TSUNAMIS	MADAGASCAR
1. The dog breed bloodhound is the only animal whose evidence is admissible in US courts. 2. Elias Howe was an American inventor who improved the sewing machine in 1846. Isaac Singer made slight modifications in the machine and a built successful business.	1) Tokyo-Yokohama, Japan 2) Manila, Philippines 3) Pearl River Delta, China 4) Osaka-Kobe, Japan 5) Jakarta, Indonesia 6) Nagoya, Japan 7) Kolkata, India	...is in the continent of Africa. Antananarivo is the capital. Over 90% of the animals in this country do not exist anywhere else on Earth. The largest predator is the fossa. It has a cat-like body and a dog-like nose, but is neither a cat nor a dog.

GROUP DISCUSSION AND CLOSING PRAYER

"Storm brings blessings, and rich fruit will be harvested later."

Henry Ward Beecher

Day 31 ~ Widow's Oil

OPENING PRAYER
READ: 2nd Kings 4:1-44

A certain woman...

1) How did Elisha help the old widow?_____
_____
_____

2) How did Elisha repay the Shunammite woman and her husband for their kindness? _____
_____

3) How did Elisha cure the stew?_____
_____

Explore God's World
MEMORY VERSES:
Exodus 34:7 "Keeping loyal love for thousands, forgiving iniquity, and transgression, and sin. But He by no means leaves the guilty unpunished, responding to the transgression of fathers by dealing with children and children's children, to the third and fourth generation."

MALACHI
Verse 1 identifies the author as Malachi.
PURPOSE
The Book of Malachi is an oracle. It is the word of the Lord to Israel through Malachi, 1:1. This was God's warning to the people, to turn back to God. As the final book of the Old Testament closes, the pronouncement of God's justice, and the promise of His restoration through the coming Messiah, is ringing in the ears of the Israelites. Four hundred years of silence ensues, ending with a similar message from God's next prophet, John the Baptist, proclaiming, "Repent, for the kingdom of heaven is near." Matthew 3:2

For Your Information

FUN FACTS	SEVEN RISKIEST CITIES PRONE TO EARTHQUAKES, HURRICANES, CYCLONES AND TSUNAMIS	MALAWI
1. You will burn more calories walking on hard dirt than on pavement. 2. Sylvester Howard Roper developed a coal-powered, two-cylinder, steam-driven, wooden motorcycle in 1867. He also developed a steam-driven car.	1) Tokyo-Yokohama, Japan 2) Manila, Philippines 3) Pearl River Delta, China 4) Osaka-Kobe, Japan 5) Jakarta, Indonesia 6) Nagoya, Japan 7) Kolkata, India	...is in the continent of Africa; Lilongwe is the capital. Malawi is among the world's least-developed and the most densely populated countries. The chambo fish, one of Malawi's favorite delicacies, is an endangered species.

GROUP DISCUSSION AND CLOSING PRAYER

"Jesus is ideal and wonderful, but you Christians - you are not like him."
Mahatma Gandhi

Day 32 ~ Naaman the Leper

OPENING PRAYER
READ: 2nd Kings 5:1-27

Now Naaman, commander...

1) Who was Naaman?_____
_____

2) What did Elisha require Naaman to do? What was Naaman's reaction?_____
_____

3) Elisha pronounced what on Gehazi?_____
_____

Explore God's World

MEMORY VERSES:

Exodus 34:7 "Keeping loyal love for thousands, forgiving iniquity, and transgression, and sin. But He by no means leaves the guilty unpunished, responding to the transgression of fathers by dealing with children and children's children, to the third and fourth generation."

For Your Information

GOSPEL OF MATTHEW

Matthew was written by the apostle Matthew. The style of the book is exactly what would be expected of a man who was once a tax collector. Because of his keen interest in accounting (18:23-24; 25:14-15), the book is very orderly and concise. Rather than writing in chronological order, Matthew arranged this Gospel into six discussions. Matthew possessed a skill that makes his writing style exciting for Christians.

PURPOSE

Matthew intends to prove to the Jews that Jesus Christ is the promised Messiah. More than any other gospel, he quotes the Old Testament to show how Jesus fulfilled the words of the Jewish prophets. Matthew describes, in detail, the lineage from King David to Jesus. Matthew's love and concern for his people are apparent through his meticulous approach to telling the gospel story.

FUN FACTS	SEVEN RISKIEST CITIES PRONE TO EARTHQUAKES, HURRICANES, CYCLONES AND TSUNAMIS	MALAYSIA
1. The only domestic animal which is not mentioned in the Bible is the cat. 2. Tens of thousands of baby girls are abandoned each year in China because of the country's one-child policy.	1) Tokyo-Yokohama, Japan; 2) Manila, Philippines; 3) Pearl River Delta, China; 4) Osaka-Kobe, Japan; 5) Jakarta, Indonesia; 6) Nagoya, Japan; 7) Kolkata, India	...is in the continent of Asia. Kuala Lumpur is the capital. The largest cave chamber in the world is the Sarawak Chamber, which can easily accommodate a Boeing 747-200. Since its independence, Malaysia has had one of the best economies in Asia.

GROUP DISCUSSION AND CLOSING PRAYER

"The only thing necessary for the triumph of evil is for good men to do nothing."

Edmund Burke

Day 33 ~ The Axe Head Made to Float

OPENING PRAYER
READ: 2nd Kings 6:1-30

And the sons of...

1) How did Elisha find the axe's head? _____

_____

2) What caused the Syrian army to be blinded, and why did they go to Samaria? _____

_____

3) How bad was the famine in Samaria, and what was the dispute between the two women? _____

_____

Explore God's World
MEMORY VERSES:

Exodus 34:7 "Keeping loyal love for thousands, forgiving iniquity, and transgression, and sin. But He by no means leaves the guilty unpunished, responding to the transgression of fathers by dealing with children and children's children, to the third and fourth generation."

GOSPEL OF MARK
Although Mark does not name its author, it is the unanimous testimony of early church fathers that the author was Mark, an associate of the Apostle Peter, and his spiritual son. 1st Peter 5:13. From Peter, he received first-hand information of the events and teachings of the Lord and preserved the information in written form. It is generally agreed that Mark is the John Mark mentioned in Acts 12:12. His mother was a wealthy and prominent Christian in the Jerusalem church. The church probably met in her home.

PURPOSE
Mark's gospel appears to be addressed to the Roman believers, particularly Gentiles. He wrote as a pastor to Christians who previously had heard and believed the Gospel. (Romans 1:8) He desired that they have a biographical story of Jesus Christ as Servant of the Lord and Savior of the world in order to strengthen their faith in the face of severe persecution, and to teach them what it meant to be His disciples.

For Your Information

FUN FACTS
1. Hammerhead sharks are born with soft heads so they won't jam their mother's birth canal.
2. Overly aggressive and overly permissive parents are equally likely to have children who bully.

SEVEN RISKIEST CITIES PRONE TO EARTHQUAKES, HURRICANES, CYCLONES AND TSUNAMIS

1) Tokyo-Yokohama, Japan
2) Manila, Philippines
3) Pearl River Delta, China
4) Osaka-Kobe, Japan
5) Jakarta, Indonesia
6) Nagoya, Japan
7) Kolkata, India

MALDIVES
...is in the continent of Asia. Male is the capital. This sovereign island country is the lowest country in the world, with an average ground level elevation of 4 feet 11 inches above sea level. Being low-lying, the authorities are concerned about the possibility of The Maldives sinking into the Indian Ocean. It is the smallest country in Asia and the smallest Muslim country in the world.

GROUP DISCUSSION AND CLOSING PRAYER

"The nice thing about egotists is that they don't talk about other people."
Lucille S. Harper

Helping Parents Develop Their Children's Love for God and for People

41

Day 34 ~ A Seven-Year Famine

OPENING PRAYER
READ: 2nd Kings 8:1-23

So Jacob was...

1) What did Gehazi tell the king about Elisha? _____
_____

2) Why was Elisha weeping? _____
_____

3) How did Jehoram walk with the Lord? _____
_____

Explore God's World
MEMORY VERSES:

Exodus 34:7 "Keeping loyal love for thousands, forgiving iniquity, and transgression, and sin. But He by no means leaves the guilty unpunished, responding to the transgression of fathers by dealing with children and children's children, to the third and fourth generation."

GOSPEL OF LUKE
From Luke 1:1-4 and Acts 1:1-3, it is clear that the same author wrote both. They are both addressed to "most excellent Theophilus," possibly a Roman dignitary. The tradition from the earliest days of the church has been that Luke, a physician and a close companion of the Paul, wrote both Luke and Acts (Colossians 4:14 and 2nd Timothy 4:11). This would make Luke the only Gentile to pen any book of Scripture.

PURPOSE
As with the other two synoptic gospels-Matthew and Mark-this book's purpose is to reveal the Lord Jesus Christ and all He "began to do and to teach until the day He was taken up to heaven" (Acts 1:1-2). Luke's gospel is unique in that it is a meticulous history - "an orderly account" (Luke 1:3) consistent with the Luke's medical mind. He often gave details that the other accounts omit. Luke's history of the life of Jesus, as the Great Physician, emphasizes His ministry to and compassion for Gentiles, Samaritans, women, children, tax collectors, sinners, and others regarded as outcasts in Israel.

For Your Information

FUN FACTS

1. The color blue is the least color in the natural foods we eat.
2. The kite originated roughly 2,500 to 3,000 years ago in China, Malaysia or Indonesia.

SEVEN RISKIEST CITIES PRONE TO EARTHQUAKES, HURRICANES, CYCLONES AND TSUNAMIS

1) Tokyo-Yokohama, Japan
2) Manila, Philippines
3) Pearl River Delta, China
4) Osaka-Kobe, Japan
5) Jakarta, Indonesia
6) Nagoya, Japan
7) Kolkata, India

MALI

...is in the continent of Africa. Bamako is the capital. It is the biggest country in West Africa and is roughly twice the size of Texas, Mali is one of the poorest nations in the world. Around 70% of the population earns less than US $1 per day.

GROUP DISCUSSION AND CLOSING PRAYER

"Wise men make proverbs, but fools repeat them."

Samuel Palmer

Day 35 ~ Week in Review

MATCH THE FOLLOWING

_____ a. Malaysia   1. A tax collector

_____ b. Malta   2. Bamako

_____ c. Kolkata   3. Unknown

_____ d. Madagascar   4. Lilongwe

_____ e. Luke   5. Kuala Lumpur

_____ f. Maldives   6. Physician

_____ g. Matthew   7. Male

_____ h. Mark   8. Valletta

_____ i. Malawi   9. Antananarivo

_____ j. Mali   9. India

TRUE OR FALSE — Circle T for true or F for false

T or F   Malawi is the world's most developed and least densely populated countries.

T or F   Matthew quotes the O.T. to show how Jesus fulfilled the words of the Jewish prophets.

T or F   Macedonia gained its independence from Yugoslavia with lot of bloodshed.

T or F   Maldives is the highest elevated country in the world.

T or F   Book of Zechariah highlighted that sin doesn't bring God's punishment.

T or F   Wise men make proverbs, but fools repeat them.

T or F   Luke is the only Gentile to pen any book of Scripture.

T or F   Malachi is the 3rd from the last book of the Old Testament.

T or F   The largest predator, the fossa, is half wolf and half tiger.

T or F   Mark focuses on Jesus Christ as Servant of the Lord and Savior of the world.

LIST THE SEVEN RISKIEST CITIES PRONE TO EARTHQUAKES, HURRICANES, CYCLONES AND TSUNAMIS

1._____   2._____

3._____   4._____

5._____   6._____

7._____

FILL IN THE BLANKS

a. The color _____ is the least _____ in the natural _____ we eat.

b. Over_____ of the_____ in Madagascar do not_____ anywhere else on _____ .

c. The _____ fish, one of Malawi's favorite _____ , is an endangered _____ .

d. Matthew intends to_____ to the_____ that Jesus is the _____ promised _____ .

e. Mali is the_____ country in _____ Africa and is roughly twice the_____ of _____ .

f. Haggai sought to _____ the people of God _____ their_____ .

g. In Macedonia, _____ Christianity is the major_____ making up_____ of the_____ .

h. This was God's _____ through Malachi to tell the_____ to turn back to_____ .

i. Malaysia has the_____ cave _____ in the world called the_____ Chamber.

j. The dog breed, _____ , is the only_____ whose evidence is _____ in US courts

MEMORIZE AND WRITE

Exodus 34:7 _____

_____

_____

THE PROPHET ELISHA & NAAMAN

Why do you believe that God had Elisha give Naaman the detailed instructions he did to be healed rather than simply having Elisha call on God's power to heal Naaman immediately?

_____

_____

_____

_____

_____

_____

_____

The Widow's Oil Coloring Activity

Note, you may make copies of this page to color if multiple family members in the same household want to color the illustration.

Day 36 ~ The Transfer of the Ark

OPENING PRAYER
READ: 1st Chronicles 13:1-14

Then Elisha spoke...

1) Where had the Ark been located?_____
_____

2) By what means did the Israelites transport the Ark? _____
_____

3) How did David feel toward God when Uzza died?_____
_____

Explore God's World

MEMORY VERSES:

Genesis 12:1-3 "Now the Lord had said to Abram: "Go from your country, from your family and from your father's house, to a land that I will show you. I will make you a great nation; I will bless you and make your name great; and you shall be a blessing. I will bless those who bless you, and I will curse him who curses you; and in you, all the families of the earth shall be blessed."

GOSPEL OF JOHN

The verses 21:20-24 describe the author as "the disciple whom Jesus loved," and for both historical and internal reasons this reference is understood to be John the Apostle, son of Zebedee (Luke 5:10).

PURPOSE

John 20:31 cites that John's purpose was to display Jesus' deity. John was seeking not only to strengthen the faith of 2nd generation believers and bring about faith in others, but also to correct a false teaching that was spreading. He emphasized Jesus Christ as "the Son of "Christ-Spirit" as coming upon the human Jesus at His baptism and leaving him at the crucifixion.

For Your Information

FUN FACTS	COUNTRIES WITH NUCLEAR WEAPONS	MALTA
1. Putting sugar directly on a wound or cut can help the healing process.	1) Russia 2) USA 3) France 4) China 5) United Kingdom 6) Pakistan 7) India	...is in the continent of Europe. Valletta is the capital. Covering just over 300 sq km, Malta is one of the world's smallest and most densely populated countries. Maltese and English are the two official languages.
2. Legos are a very popular interlocking plastic toy. The LEGO toy company was founded by Ole Kirk Christiansen of Denmark in 1932.		

GROUP DISCUSSION AND CLOSING PRAYER

"The weak can never forgive. Forgiveness is the attribute of the strong."

Mahatma Gandhi

Day 37 ~ The Arrival and Installation of the Ark

David built houses...

1) David appointed whom as the sole transporters of the Ark of God?_____
_____

2) Where was the Ark placed, and what was offered unto God?_____
_____

3) What responsibility was given to Asaph and his brothers?_____
_____

Explore God's World

MEMORY VERSES:

Genesis 12:1-3 "Now the Lord had said to Abram: "Go from your country, from your family and from your father's house, to a land that I will show you. I will make you a great nation; I will bless you and make your name great; and you shall be a blessing. I will bless those who bless you, and I will curse him who curses you; and in you, all the families of the earth shall be blessed.""

ACTS

The book does not specifically identify its author. From Luke 1:1-4 and Acts 1:1-3, it is clear that the same author wrote both books.

PURPOSE

It was written to provide a history of the early church. The emphasis is on the importance of the day of Pentecost and the empowerment disciples needed to be effective witnesses for Jesus Christ. Acts records the apostles being witnesses for Christ's in Jerusalem, Judea, Samaria, and to the rest of the surrounding world. Acts sheds light on the gift of the Holy Spirit, who empowers, guides, teaches, and serves as our Counselor. Reading Acts, we are enlightened and encouraged by the many miracles that were performed during this time by the disciples Peter, John, and Paul. The importance of obedience to God's Word and the transformation that occurs as a result of knowing Christ are emphasized. There are many references to those who rejected the gospel's truth preached by the disciples. The lust for power, greed, and many other vices of the devil are evidenced in the book of Acts.

For Your Information

FUN FACTS	COUNTRIES WITH NUCLEAR WEAPONS	MARSHALL ISLANDS
1. Earnest V. Wright wrote a 50,000 word book titled "Gatsby", without using the letter "e." 2. Galileo invented the thermometer in 1609, and also was the first person to use a telescope.	1) Russia 2) USA 3) France 4) China 5) United Kingdom 6) Pakistan 7) India	...is in the continent of Australia (Oceanic). Majuro is the capital. The only indigenous land mammal in the islands is the Polynesian rat. The two official languages are Marshallese and English. The important crops are coconuts, tomatoes, melons, and breadfruit.

GROUP DISCUSSION AND CLOSING PRAYER

"Pray and let God worry."
Martin Luther

Day 38 ~ David's Preparation for Building of the Temple

OPENING PRAYER

READ: 1st Chronicles 22:2-19

Then David said...

1) What was the purpose of building the temple?_____
_____

2) What preparations and materials did David make for the building of the temple?_____
_____

3) What did God promise to Solomon for his reign as a king? _____
_____

Explore God's World

MEMORY VERSES:

Genesis 12:1-3 "Now the Lord had said to Abram: "Go from your country, from your family and from your father's house, to a land that I will show you. I will make you a great nation; I will bless you and make your name great; and you shall be a blessing. I will bless those who bless you, and I will curse him who curses you; and in you, all the families of the earth shall be blessed.""

ROMANS

Verse 1 identifies the author as the apostle Paul. Romans 16:22 indicates that Paul used a man named Tertius to transcribe his words.

PURPOSE

Paul's purpose was to proclaim the glory of the Lord Jesus Christ by teaching doctrine, edifying, and encouraging the believers who would receive his letter. Of particular concern to Paul were those to whom this letter was written; those in Rome who were "loved by God and called to be saints" (Romans 1:7). Because he was a Roman citizen, he had a unique passion for those in the assembly of believers in Rome. Since he had not, to this point, visited the church in Rome, this letter also served as his introduction to them.

For Your Information

FUN FACTS	COUNTRIES WITH NUCLEAR WEAPONS	MEXICO
1. Garrett Augustus Morgan invented a traffic signal and developed the gas mask. 2. Richard G. Drew (1899-1980) invented masking tape and clear adhesive tape. Drew was an engineer for the 3M company (the Minnesota Mining and Manufacturing).	1) Russia 2) USA 3) France 4) China 5) United Kingdom 6) Pakistan 7) India	...is in the continent of North America. Mexico City is the capital. Mexico is home to a very rare rabbit called the volcano. Mexico is the 11th most populous country and the most populous Spanish-speaking country in the world and the second most populous country in Latin America.

GROUP DISCUSSION AND CLOSING PRAYER

"I've learned that people will forget what you said, people will forget what you did, but people will never forget how you made them feel."

Maya Angelou

Day 39 ~ The Commencement and Cessation of the Temple

Now in the second...

OPENING PRAYER
READ: Ezra 3:8-13 and 4:1-5

1) What was the age required to work in the temple?_____

_____

2) Why did the old priests and Levites cry out loudly?_____

_____

3) What were the attitudes of Zerubbabel and Jeshua in rebuilding the temple?_____

_____

Explore God's World

MEMORY VERSES:

Genesis 12:1-3 "Now the Lord had said to Abram: "Go from your country, from your family and from your father's house, to a land that I will show you. I will make you a great nation; I will bless you and make your name great; and you shall be a blessing. I will bless those who bless you, and I will curse him who curses you; and in you, all the families of the earth shall be blessed."

1ST CORINTHIANS
Verse 1 identifies the author as the apostle Paul of 1st Corinthians.

PURPOSE
Apostle Paul founded the church in Corinth. A few years after leaving the church, he heard disturbing reports that Corinthian were full of pride, excusing sexual immorality, spiritual gifts were being used improperly, and there was rampant misunderstanding of key Christian doctrines. The apostle Paul wrote his first letter to the Corinthians in an attempt to restore the Corinthian church to its foundation in Jesus Christ.

For Your Information

FUN FACTS	COUNTRIES WITH NUCLEAR WEAPONS	MAURITANIA
1. Blood collection centers often run short of red blood cells types O and B. 2. There is enough concrete in the Hoover Dam to pave a two lane highway from San Francisco to New York.	1) Russia 2) USA 3) France 4) China 5) United Kingdom 6) Pakistan 7) India	...is in the continent of Africa. Nouakchott is the capital. Aside from Madagascar, Mauritania is the only country that does not use a decimal currency. Nearly 40% of the country's exports is made up of iron ore due to its abundant availability in the region.

GROUP DISCUSSION AND CLOSING PRAYER

"God has given us two hands, one to receive with and the other to give with."

Billy Graham

Day 40 ~ The Resumption of the Temple

OPENING PRAYER
READ: Ezra 5:1-17

Then the Prophet...

1) How were Zerubbabel and Jeshua able to start rebuilding the temple again?_____

_____

2) What did King Cyrus do for Israel? _____

_____

3) What was Tattenai's request of King Darius?_____

_____

Explore God's World

MEMORY VERSES:

Genesis 12:1-3 "Now the Lord had said to Abram: "Go from your country, from your family and from your father's house, to a land that I will show you. I will make you a great nation; I will bless you and make your name great; and you shall be a blessing. I will bless those who bless you, and I will curse him who curses you; and in you, all the families of the earth shall be blessed."

2ND CORINTHIANS
Verse 1 identifies the author of 2nd Corinthians as Paul, possibly along with Timothy.

PURPOSE
The church in Corinth began in A.D. 52 when Paul visited there on his 2nd missionary journey. It was then that he stayed one and a half years, the 1st time he was allowed to stay in one place as long as he wished. A record of this visit and the establishment of the church are found in Acts 18:1-18.

For Your Information

FUN FACTS	COUNTRIES WITH NUCLEAR WEAPONS	MAURITIUS
1. After eating too much, the sense of hearing becomes less sharp. 2. An acre of trees can remove about 13 tons of dust and gases from the surrounding environment every year.	1) Russia 2) USA 3) France 4) China 5) United Kingdom 6) Pakistan 7) India	...is in the continent of Africa. Port Louis is the capital. The island nation is multiethnic, multi-religious and multicultural. Most citizens are multilingual, speaking English, French, Creole, and Asian languages. Mauritius has no exploitable natural resources and thus depends on imported petroleum products.

GROUP DISCUSSION AND CLOSING PRAYER

"Advice is what we ask for when we already know the answer, but wish we didn't."

Erica Jong

Day 41 ~ The Completion of the Temple

Then King Darius...

OPENING PRAYER
READ: Ezra 6:1-22

1) Why were the archives in Babylon searched? _____
_____

2) What orders did King Darius give to Tattenai and his associates? _____
_____

3) Why were the priests and the Levites assigned to the temple? _____
_____

Explore God's World

MEMORY VERSES:

Genesis 12:1-3 "Now the Lord had said to Abram: "Go from your country, from your family and from your father's house, to a land that I will show you. I will make you a great nation; I will bless you and make your name great; and you shall be a blessing. I will bless those who bless you, and I will curse him who curses you; and in you, all the families of the earth shall be blessed.""

GALATIANS

Verse 1 clearly identifies the Apostle Paul as the writer of Galatians.

PURPOSE

The churches in Galatia were formed partly of converted Jews and partly of Gentile converts. Paul asserts his apostolic character and the doctrines he taught, that he might confirm the Galatian churches in the faith of Christ. The subject is mainly the same as is discussed in Romans, that is, the importance of justification by faith alone. In this epistle, however, it states that men are justified by faith without the works of the Law of Moses. Galatians was written as a protest against corruption of the gospel of Christ. The essential truth of justification by faith rather than by the works of the law had been obscured by the Judaizers' claim that believers in Christ must keep the law, if they expected to be perfect before God. When Paul learned that this teaching had begun to penetrate the Galatian churches, thus separating them from their heritage of liberty, he wrote the impassioned response contained in this epistle.

For Your Information

FUN FACTS	COUNTRIES WITH NUCLEAR WEAPONS	MICRONESIA
1. In 1967, the 1st successful heart transplant was performed in Cape Town, South Africa. 2. Joseph Gayetty invented toilet paper in 1857. His new toilet paper was composed of flat sheets. Before his invention, people tore pages out of mail order catalogs.	1) Russia 2) USA 3) France 4) China 5) United Kingdom 6) Pakistan 7) India	...is in the continent of Australia (Oceanic). Palikir is the capital. The Federated States of Micronesia, comprising thousands of small islands in the western Pacific, derives its name from the Greek milkos, "small" and nesos, "island." The primary income comes from the sale of fishing rights to foreign nations that harvest tuna using huge purse seiners.

GROUP DISCUSSION AND CLOSING PRAYER

"I have often regretted my speech, never my silence."

Xenocrates

Day 42 ~ Week in Review

MEMORIZE AND WRITE

Genesis 12:1-3 _____

_____

_____

_____

TRUE OR FALSE — Circle T for true or F for false

T or F   The only indigenous land mammal is the Polynesian dog.

T or F   Marshall Islands is famous for Polynesian whale.

T or F   Romans was written to the Roman Empire.

T or F   John's purpose that you may believe that Jesus is the Christ, the Son of God.

T or F   The Greek word *mikrós* means "small" and *nēsos* means "island."

T or F   Acts doesn't shed light on the Holy Spirit but rather on Paul's missionary work.

T or F   Galatians was written as a protest is against corruption of the gospel of Christ.

T or F   Malta has two official languages, Maltese and English.

T or F   Mauritius has a lot of natural resources and abundance of petroleum products.

T or F   You must be the change you wish to see in the world.

T or F   Corinthians were full of pride and were excusing sexual immorality.

MATCH THE FOLLOWING

_____ a. Mauritius   1. Nouakchott

_____ b. Romans   2. Pakistan and China

_____ c. Mexico   3. Unknown

_____ d. Marshall Islands   4. Son of Zebedee

_____ e. Micronesia   5. Paul

_____ f. Nuclear Weapons   6. Mexico City

_____ g. Malta   7. Majuro

_____ h. Acts   8. Port Louis

_____ i. John   9. Valletta

_____ j. Mauritania   9. Palikir

FILL IN THE BLANKS

a. The volcano_____,the world's second _____rabbit, lives in the _____of Mexico.

b. Micronesia_____ its name from the _____ *milkos*, "small and _____, island".

c. Putting sugar_____on a_____or cut can help the _____process.

d. John emphasized Jesus_____as "the_____of _____," fully_____and fully man.

e. Romans 16:_____indicates that Paul used a _____name_____ to transcribe his words.

f. The_____official _____of Marshall Islands are Marshallese and _____.

g. Malta is one of the_____smallest and most _____populated_____.

h. Ernst V._____wrote a _____word book titled "Gatsby" without _____the letter "e."

i. Acts was_____to provide a_____of the early_____.

j. Mauritius has no_____natural resources and thus_____on imported _____products.

LIST THE COUNTRIES WITH NUCLEAR WEAPONS

_____

_____

_____

_____

THE ARK & THE TEMPLE

What were some of the specific instructions that God gave to King David and the Israelites about the Ark and the Temple?

_____

_____

_____

_____

_____

_____

_____

_____

The Temple Courtyard Coloring Activity

*Note, you may make copies of this page to color if multiple family members in
the same household want to color the illustration.*

Day 43 ~ The Prayer and Planning of Nehemiah Concerning Jerusalem

OPENING PRAYER
READ: Nehemiah 1:1-11 and 2:11-20

The words of Nehemiah...

1) What report did Hanani and his men give to Nehemiah?_____
_____

2) Nehemiah saw what through the Valley Gate to the Serpent Well and the Refuse Gate?_____
_____

3) From where did Nehemiah receive his encouragement to rebuild Jerusalem?_____
_____

Explore God's World

MEMORY VERSES:

Genesis 17:3-4 Then Abram fell on his face, and God talked with him, saying: "As for Me, behold, My covenant is with you, and you shall be a father of many nations."

GALATIANS
Verse 1 identifies the author of Ephesians as the apostle Paul.
PURPOSE
Paul intended that all who long for Christ-like maturity would receive this writing. Enclosed in the Book is the discipline needed to develop into a true believer of God. Furthermore, a study in Ephesians will help to fortify and establish the believer so he can fulfill the purpose and calling God has given him. The aim of this epistle is to confirm and to equip a maturing church, as well as present a balanced view of the body of Christ and its importance in God's economy.

For Your Information

FUN FACTS	THE TOP FIVE MILK PRODUCING COWS	MOLDOVA
1. Jesse W. Reno was an American inventor who developed the first escalator in 1891. 2. Jonas Salk formulated a vaccine against the devastating disease polio, also called infantile paralysis.	1) **Holstein:** Produces 12,000 kg per year, Israel and Netherlands 2) **Norwegian Red:** Produces 10,000 kg per year, Norway 3) **Kostroma Cattle Breed:** Produces 10,000 kg per year, Russia 4) **Brown Swiss:** Produces 9,000 kg per year, Switzerland 5) **Swedish Red Cattle:** Produces 8000 kg per year Sweden	...is in the continent of Europe. Chisinau is the capital. The official language is Romanian. With its long history of winemaking, Moldova is the 7th largest wine exporter worldwide. Imports from Russia are largely petroleum, coal, and natural gas.

GROUP DISCUSSION AND CLOSING PRAYER

"Knowledge speaks, but wisdom listens."
Jimi Hendrix

Day 44 ~ Rebuilding the Wall

OPENING PRAYER
READ: Nehemiah 3:1-25

Then Eliashib the...

1) What project did the Israelites work on?_____
_____
_____

2) Who were the people involved in rebuilding Jerusalem?_____
_____

3) How did the Priests and Levites set an example for all the Israelites?_____
_____

Explore God's World

Genesis 17:3-4 Then Abram fell on his face, and God talked with him, saying: "As for Me, behold, My covenant is with you, and you shall be a father of many nations."

PHILIPPIANS
Verse 1 identifies the author of Philippians as Paul, likely along with the help of Timothy.
PURPOSE
One of Paul's prison epistles, written in Rome. It was at Philippi, which the apostle visited on his second missionary journey (Acts 16:12), that Lydia, the Philippian jailer, and his family were converted to Christ. Now, some a few years later, the church was well established, as may be inferred from its addressing "bishops (elders) and deacons" (Philippians 1:1)

For Your Information

FUN FACTS
1. If you Google "Zerg rush" Google will eat up the search engine.
2. Samuel Finley Breese Morse (1791-1872) was inventor and painter. He built the first American telegraph. It was developed independently in Europe around 1835.

THE TOP FIVE MILK PRODUCING COWS
1) **Holstein**: Produces 12,000 kg per year, Israel and Netherlands
2) **Norwegian Red**: Produces 10,000 kg per year, Norway
3) **Kostroma Cattle Breed**: Produces 10,000 kg per year, Russia
4) **Brown Swiss**: Produces 9,000 kg per year, Switzerland
5) **Swedish Red Cattle**: Produces 8000 kg per year Sweden

MONACO
...is in the continent of Europe; Monaco is the capital. It is the 2nd smallest country in the world. The state has no income tax, has low business taxes, and is well known for being a tax haven. Monaco has no navy or air force. Rugby is the national sport.

GROUP DISCUSSION AND CLOSING PRAYER

"It is always the simple that produces the marvelous."

Amelia Barr

Day 45 ~ Opposition

OPENING PRAYER
READ: Nehemiah 4:1-23

But it so happened...

1) Why did Sanballat become angry with the Jews? How did he treat them? _____
_____
_____

2) What were the challenges the men faced in building the wall (especially in verses 15-18)?_____
_____

3) Why did they take off their clothes for washing only?_____
_____

Explore God's World

Genesis 17:3-4 Then Abram fell on his face, and God talked with him, saying: "As for Me, behold, My covenant is with you, and you shall be a father of many nations."

COLOSSIANS
The apostle Paul was the primary writer (1:3). Timothy is also given some credit (1:1).

PURPOSE
Colossians is a mini-ethics course, addressing every area of Christian life. Paul progresses from the individual life to the home and family, from work to the way we should treat others. The theme is the sufficiency of our Lord, Jesus Christ, in meeting our needs in every area.

For Your Information

FUN FACTS	THE TOP FIVE MILK PRODUCING COWS	MONGOLIA
1. The idea to divide the Earth into time zones was proposed by Sir Sandford Fleming. 2. The average high school student today has the same level of anxiety as the average psychiatric patient in the early 1950's.	1) **Holstein**: Produces 12,000 kg/yr, Israel and Netherlands 2) **Norwegian Red**: Produces 10,000 kg/yr, Norway 3) **Kostroma Cattle Breed**: Produces 10,000 kg/yr, Russia 4) **Brown Swiss**: Produces 9,000 kg/yr, Switzerland 5) **Swedish Red Cattle**: Produces 8000 kg/yr, Sweden	...is in the continent of Asia. Ulaanbaatar is the capital. Kumis is an ancient beverage that originated here. It is a fermented, raw, unpasteurized mare's milk made over the course of hours or days. The finished product contains between 0.7 and 2.5% alcohol. Mongolian is the official language while Russian is the most frequently spoken foreign language.

GROUP DISCUSSION AND CLOSING PRAYER

"You must do the things you think you cannot do."

Eleanor Roosevelt

Day 46 ~ The Conflict of the Jewish People

OPENING PRAYER
READ: Nehemiah 5:1-19

And there was a great...

1) What was the outcry of these different people? _____
_____
_____

2) Why was Nehemiah angry in verse 6? _____
_____

3) What did the previous governor do wrong? _____
_____

Explore God's World

Genesis 17:3-4 Then Abram fell on his face, and God talked with him, saying: "As for Me, behold, My covenant is with you, and you shall be a father of many nations."

1ST THESSALONIANS
Verse 1 indicates apostle Paul as author, probably along with Silas and Timothy.
PURPOSE
In the church of Thessalonica there was some misunderstanding about the return of Christ. Paul desired to clarify the subject in his letter, which gives instruction in holy living

For Your Information

FUN FACTS	THE TOP FIVE MILK PRODUCING COWS	MONTENEGRO
1. New Jersey is home to the world's 1st drive-in movie theater. 2. Sweat itself is odorless; bacteria on the skin mingles with sweat to produce body odor.	1) **Holstein**: Produces 12,000 kg per year, Israel and Netherlands 2) **Norwegian Red**: Produces 10,000 kg per year, Norway 3) **Kostroma Cattle Breed**: Produces 10,000 kg per year, Russia 4) **Brown Swiss**: Produces 9,000 kg per year, Switzerland 5) **Swedish Red Cattle**: Produces 8000 kg per year Sweden	...is in the continent of Europe. Podgorica is the capital. The name of the country means "Black Mountain." The official language is Montenegrin. Serbian, Bosnian, Albanian, and Croatian are also spoken. Elementary education is free and compulsory for ages 6 to 14.

GROUP DISCUSSION AND CLOSING PRAYER

"Our Creator has always known of us and has always loved us."

Michael Mannia, The Conditioned Mind

Day 47 ~ Renewed Opposition

OPENING PRAYER
READ: Nehemiah 6:1-19

Now it happened...

1) Why did Sanballat and his associates want to summon Nehemiah?_____
_____
_____

2) How did Nehemiah respond to Sanballat's accusations?_____
_____

3) Why did Tobiah continue to send letters to Nehemiah?_____
_____

Explore God's World

Genesis 17:3-4 Then Abram fell on his face, and God talked with him, saying: "As for Me, behold, My covenant is with you, and you shall be a father of many nations."

2ND THESSALONIANS
Verse 1 indicates apostle Paul as author, probably along with Silas and Timothy.
PURPOSE
The church in Thessalonica still had some misconceptions about the Day of the Lord. They thought it had come already, so they had stopped their work for the Lord. Believers were being persecuted severely. Paul wrote to clear up misconceptions and to comfort them

For Your Information

FUN FACTS

1. You can change your language on Facebook to "Pirate."
2. Found in the Pacific Ocean, the Marianas Trench is the deepest part of the world's oceans.

THE TOP FIVE MILK PRODUCING COWS

1) **Holstein**: Produces 12,000 kg per year, Israel and Netherlands
2) **Norwegian Red**: Produces 10,000 kg per year, Norway
3) **Kostroma Cattle Breed**: Produces 10,000 kg per year, Russia
4) **Brown Swiss**: Produces 9,000 kg per year, Switzerland
5) **Swedish Red Cattle**: Produces 8000 kg per year Sweden

MOROCCO

...is in the continent of Africa. Rabat is the capital. Declining to eat meat and handling food with the left hand are considered impolite. Traditionally, the belief is that the liver, not the heart, is the symbol of love.

GROUP DISCUSSION AND CLOSING PRAYER

"What lies behind you and what lies in front of you pales in comparison to what lies inside of you."

Jenari Skye

Day 48 ~ The Restoration of the People

OPENING PRAYER
READ: Nehemiah 13:1-27

On that day they...

1) What did the Israelites discover when they read the book of Moses at the celebration?_____
_____

_____

2) How did Nehemiah react to Eliashib's sin?_____
_____

3) Why did Elisha curse, strike, and pull the hair of the Jews who had foreign wives?_____
_____

Explore God's World

Genesis 17:3-4 Then Abram fell on his face, and God talked with him, saying: "As for Me, behold, My covenant is with you, and you shall be a father of many nations."

1ST TIMOTHY
Verse 1 states apostle Paul as the author of 1st Timothy.
PURPOSE
Paul wrote to Timothy to encourage him in his responsibility for overseeing the work of the Ephesian church and possibly the other churches in the province of Asia (Timothy 1:3). This letter lays the foundation for ordaining elders (Timothy 3:1-7) and provides guidance for ordaining people into offices of the church (Timothy 3:8-13). It is a leadership manual for church organization and administration.

For Your Information

FUN FACTS	THE TOP FIVE MILK PRODUCING COWS	MOZAMBIQUE
1. The Chinese used fingerprints as a method of identification as far back as 700 AD. 2. In Japan, 90% of cell phones are waterproof because youngsters use them even in the shower.	1) **Holstein**: Produces 12,000 kg per year, Israel and Netherlands 2) **Norwegian Red**: Produces 10,000 kg per year, Norway 3) **Kostroma Cattle Breed**: Produces 10,000 kg per year, Russia 4) **Brown Swiss**: Produces 9,000 kg per year, Switzerland 5) **Swedish Red Cattle**: Produces 8000 kg per year Sweden	...is in the continent of Africa. Maputo is the capital. Some of the richest coral reefs are found here. The only official language is Portuguese. Common native languages include Swahili, Makhuwa, and Sena. The currency is the New Metical.

GROUP DISCUSSION AND CLOSING PRAYER

"No one can make you feel inferior without your consent."

Eleanor Roosevelt, This is My Story

Day 49 ~ Week in Review

MEMORIZE AND WRITE

Genesis 17:3-4 _____

_____

_____

TRUE OR FALSE — Circle T for true or F for false

T or F   Monaco is the 7th smallest country in the world.

T or F   The Church of Thessalonica was an exemplarily in their walk with Christ.

T or F   Philippians was written when Paul was in Jerusalem.

T or F   The aim of Ephesians is to confirm and to equip a maturing church.

T or F   Montenegro means "dark brown mountain."

T or F   The theme of Colossians is how one gets super rich being a Christian.

T or F   Moldova's official language is Romanian.

T or F   The currency of Mozambique is the Euro.

T or F   In Morocco the liver, not the heart, is the symbol of love.

MATCH THE FOLLOWING

_____ a. Montenegro   1. Ulaanbaatar

_____ b. Mozambique   2. Prison epistles

_____ c. Swedish Red Cattle   3. Paul

_____ d. Colossians   4. No income tax

_____ e. 1st Timothy   5. Podgorica

_____ f. Mongolia   6. An instruction in holy living

_____ g. Morocco   7. Leadership manual

_____ h. Monaco   8. Chisinau

_____ i. 1st Thessalonians   9. Produces 8000 kg per year

_____ j. Moldova   10. Every area of Christian life

_____ k. Philippians   11. Rabat

_____ l. Ephesians   12. Maputo

LIST THE TOP FIVE MILK PRODUCING COWS

1. _____   2. _____

3. _____   4. _____

5. _____

FILL IN THE BLANKS

a. Monaco has no_____or air force. _____is the national_____.

b. Colossians is a _____-_____course, addressing_____area of_____life.

c. If you Google "_____rush" _____will eat up the_____engine.

d. With its long history of _____, Moldova is the 7th_____wine exporter_____.

e. "Kumis" is a_____raw unpasteurized_____milk made over the_____of hours or days.

f. In the_____ of Thessalonica there was some _____about the_____of_____.

g. Jesse W. _____was an_____inventor who_____the first_____in 1891.

h. In Morocco_____to eat meat and _____ food with the left hand are_____impolite.

i. In Montenegro the official _____is Montenegrin; also_____are Serbian, _____, Albanian and_____.

i. Mozambique have _____of the_____coral _____.

REBUILDING THE TEMPLE

What were some of the specific challenges that the men faced as they were rebuilding the Temple?

_____

_____

_____

_____

_____

_____

_____

_____

_____

_____

Bible Word Search

```
P H B V C E D H E F U S I B J
Z V N E P H D E N U N Y J I V
O V T Z U R A X Q O Q O E H C
U R I S R A E L I T E S R S H
H O O J L S N T L S J Q U A Q
A G E N L E A O A E A M S I C
I J A L R S V N M U N W A L L
B E A T U E B I D M Y G L E O
O W F C E A V L T N U E E V T
T S C L L O I O G E A S M S H
T A T L O U L L G E S Y E A E
R R A J B P R I E S T S N N S
A T S E Y R C T U O J A R O I
T W R M O S E S C P N N Z N D
H A I M E H E N W I J N B M Q
```

ACCUSATIONS	CHALLENGES	CLOTHES
ELIASHIB	GATE	GOVERNOR
HANANI	ISRAELITES	JERUSALEM
JEWS	LEVITES	MOSES
NEHEMIAH	OUTCRY	PRIESTS
REBUILD	SANBALLAT	SUMMON
TOBIAH	WALLS	

Day 50 ~ A Defeated Queen and a Discovered Queen

OPENING PRAYER

READ: Esther 1:1-13 and 2:1-18

Now it came to pass...

1) Who attended the King's banquet? _____

_____

_____

2) How did King Ahasuerus react to Vashti's disobedience? _____

_____

3) How did Esther become queen? _____

_____

Explore God's World

MEMORY VERSES:

Genesis 17:5-6 No longer shall your name be called Abram, but your name shall be Abraham; for I have made you a father of many nations. I will make you exceedingly fruitful; and I will make nations of you, and kings shall come from you.

2ND TIMOTHY

Verse 1 states apostle Paul as the author of 2nd Timothy.

PURPOSE

Imprisoned in Rome yet again, the apostle Paul felt lonely and abandoned. Paul recognized that his earthly life was likely coming to an end soon. Looking past his own circumstances, Paul wanted to use his last words to encourage Timothy and all other believers to persevere in their faith (2nd Timothy 3:14) and proclaim the gospel of Jesus Christ (2nd Timothy 4:2).

For Your Information

FUN FACTS	THE SEVEN MOST DENSELY POPULATED US STATES	MYANMAR (BURMA)
1. Donald Duck's full name is Donald Fauntleroy Duck. 2. Vampire bats are one of the few mammals known to adopt orphans and share food with less fortunate roost mates.	1) California 2) Texas 3) New York 4) Florida 5) Illinois 6) Pennsylvania 7) Ohio	...is in continent of Asia. Naypyidaw is the capital. Formerly known as Burma, this country is the world's 40th largest country and the 2nd largest in Southeast Asia. Jade, gems, oil, natural gas, and other mineral resources are its assets. The major agricultural product is rice.

GROUP DISCUSSION AND CLOSING PRAYER

"We know what we are, but know not what we may be."

William Shakespeare

Day 51 ~ Haman's Exaltation and Hatred of Mordecai

OPENING PRAYER

READ: Esther 3:1-15 and 4:10-17

After these things...

1) How did King Ahasuerus honor Haman? _____
_____
_____

2) How did Esther discover the reason behind Mordecai's grief?_____
_____

3) What request did Esther ask of Mordecai and other Jews? _____
_____

Explore God's World

MEMORY VERSES:

Genesis 17:5-6 No longer shall your name be called Abram, but your name shall be Abraham; for I have made you a father of many nations. I will make you exceedingly fruitful; and I will make nations of you, and kings shall come from you.

TITUS
Verse 1 identifies the apostle Paul as the author of Titus.
PURPOSE
Titus is known as one of the pastoral epistles, as are the two letters to Timothy. This epistle was written to encourage his brother in the faith, Titus. Titus had been left in Crete to lead the church which Paul had established on one of his missionary journeys (Titus 1:5). Titus is instructed in the qualifications of church leaders, as well as warned of the ungodly reputation of the Cretans (Titus 1:12).

For Your Information

FUN FACTS	THE SEVEN MOST DENSELY POPULATED US STATES	NEPAL
1. "Dimension 6" was the original name for "Nike." 2. Real diamonds have a radiolucent molecular structure, which means that they don't appear in x-ray images.	1) California 2) Texas 3) New York 4) Florida 5) Illinois 6) Pennsylvania 7) Ohio	...is in the continent of Asia. Kathmandu is the capital. The country has close ties with both of its neighbors, India and China. The Nepalese may work in India without legal restrictions Lumbini is one of the holiest places, and is the birthplace of Lord Gautama Buddha. Most of the population follows Hinduism, which shares the same common temples and worship common deities as Buddhists.

GROUP DISCUSSION AND CLOSING PRAYER

"It is in your moments of decision that your destiny is shaped."

Tony Robin

Day 52 ~ The First Banquet: Mordecai's Reward

Now it happened that...

OPENING PRAYER

READ: Esther 5:1-14 and 6:1-14

1) What was the conversation between the King and Esther? _____
_____

2) What was Haman's plot against Mordecai? _____
_____

3) Why was Haman forced to honor Mordecai? _____
_____

Explore God's World

MEMORY VERSES:

Genesis 17:5-6 No longer shall your name be called Abram, but your name shall be Abraham; for I have made you a father of many nations. I will make you exceedingly fruitful; and I will make nations of you, and kings shall come from you.

PHILEMON
Verse 1 states Paul as the author..

PURPOSE
Philemon, the shortest of Paul's writings, deals with the practice of slavery. The letter suggests that Paul was in prison at the time of the writing. Philemon was a slave owner who hosted a church in his home. During the time of Paul's ministry in Ephesus, Philemon had likely journeyed to the city, heard Paul's preaching, and become a Christian. The slave Onesimus robbed his master, Philemon, and ran away, making his way to Rome and to Paul. Because Onesimus was still the property of Philemon, Paul wrote to smooth the way for his return to his master. Through Paul's witnessing to him, Onesimus had become a Christian (Philemon 10), and Paul wanted Philemon to accept Onesimus as a brother in Christ and not merely as a slave

For Your Information

FUN FACTS	THE SEVEN MOST DENSELY POPULATED US STATES	NAURU
1. Ostriches can run faster than horses, and the males can roar like lion. 2. In Germany, publicly denying the holocaust earns a prison sentence.	1) California 2) Texas 3) New York 4) Florida 5) Illinois 6) Pennsylvania 7) Ohio	…is in the continent of Australia (Oceanic). Yaren is the capital. Formerly known as Pleasant Island, Nauru means "I go to the beach." The Polynesian rat, cats, dogs, pigs, and chickens have been introduced to Nauru from ships. Nauru is the smallest state in the South Pacific and the third smallest state by area in the world.

GROUP DISCUSSION AND CLOSING PRAYER

"Hope is some extraordinary spiritual grace that God gives us to control our fears, not to oust them."

Vincent McNabb

Day 53 ~ The Second Banquet

OPENING PRAYER
READ: Esther 7:1-10

So the king and...

1) What was the king's response when he learned the truth about Haman?_____
_____

2) Describe Haman's reaction when his wicked plan was exposed?_____
_____

3) How did the eunuch's revelation to the king further indict Haman?_____
_____

Explore God's World

MEMORY VERSES:

Genesis 17:5-6 No longer shall your name be called Abram, but your name shall be Abraham; for I have made you a father of many nations. I will make you exceedingly fruitful; and I will make nations of you, and kings shall come from you.

HEBREWS

Some include Hebrews among the Apostle Paul's writings, but the certain identity of the author is unknown. Paul's customary salutation, common to his other works, is missing. The writer of this epistle relied upon knowledge and information of actual eye-witnesses of Christ. (Hebrews 2:3) makes Pauline authorship doubtful. Some attribute this book to Luke. Others suggest it may have been written by Apollos, Barnabas, Silas, Philip, or Aquila and Priscilla. Hebrews speaks with the same canonical authority as the other sixty-five books of the Bible.

PURPOSE

The late Dr. Walter Martin, founder of the Christian Research Institute and writer of the best-selling book Kingdom of the Cults, quipped in his usual tongue-in-cheek manner that the Book of Hebrews was written by a Hebrew to other Hebrews telling the Hebrews to stop acting like Hebrews. Many of the early Jewish believers were slipping back into the rites and rituals of Judaism in order to escape the mounting persecution. This letter is an exhortation to those persecuted believers to continue in the grace of Jesus Christ

For Your Information

FUN FACTS	THE SEVEN MOST DENSELY POPULATED US STATES	NAMIBIA
1. "Phonophobia" is the fear of loud sounds, voices or of one's own voice. 2. Adolf Hitler's party, which came into power in 1933, was known as Nazi Party.	1) California 2) Texas 3) New York 4) Florida 5) Illinois 6) Pennsylvania 7) Ohio	...is in the continent of Africa. Windhoek is the capital. Namibia is known as the "Gem of Africa." The Welwitschia Mirabilis, a fossil plant found in the Namib Desert, has a lifespan that can reach 2,000 years. The Namib Desert is known to be the world's oldest desert.

GROUP DISCUSSION AND CLOSING PRAYER

"If we did all the things we are capable of, we would literally astound ourselves."
Thomas A. Edison

Day 54 ~ Mordecai Honored

OPENING PRAYER
READ: Esther 8:1-17

Then the Lord said...

1) What did Esther gain from risking her life to stand up for her people?_____
_____

2) How was Mordecai honored by the king?_____
_____

3) How did Mordecai ensure that all Jews would be able to protect themselves?_____
_____

Explore God's World

MEMORY VERSES:

Genesis 17:5-6 No longer shall your name be called Abram, but your name shall be Abraham; for I have made you a father of many nations. I will make you exceedingly fruitful; and I will make nations of you, and kings shall come from you.

JAMES

The author is James, also called James the Just, who is thought to be the brother of Jesus Christ (Matt. 13:55; Mark 6:3). James was not a believer (John 7:3-5) until after Jesus' resurrection (Acts 1:14; 1st Corinthians 15:7; Galatians 1:19). He became the head of the Jerusalem church and is mentioned as a pillar of the church (Galatians 2:9).

PURPOSE

"Antinomianism" held that faith in Christ completely frees one from all O.T. laws, legalism, secular law, and Mosaic morality law. Martin Luther detested this letter and called it "the epistle of straw". He failed to recognize that James' teaching on works did not contradict, but complemented Paul's teaching on faith. Paul concentrates on justification with God. James' concentrates on the works that exemplify that justification. James emphasizes that good actions will naturally flow from those who are filled with the Spirit; yet he questions whether someone may not have a saving faith, if the fruit of the Spirit cannot be seen, as Paul describes (Galatians 5:22-23)

For Your Information

FUN FACTS	THE SEVEN MOST DENSELY POPULATED US STATES	NEW ZEALAND
1. Golden Sikh Temple in Amritsar is India's largest Gurdwara. 2. Baseball and cricket are the only major sports where the defense has the ball.	1) California 2) Texas 3) New York 4) Florida 5) Illinois 6) Pennsylvania 7) Ohio	...is in the continent of Australia (Oceania); Wellington is the capital. The country is home to the world's smallest Hectors Dolphin and the rare Hookers Sea Lion. English, Maori, and NZ Sign Language are the official languages. The adult literacy rate is 99%.

GROUP DISCUSSION AND CLOSING PRAYER

"Your attitude, not your aptitude, will determine your altitude."

Zig Ziglar

Day 55 ~ The Jews Destroy Their Enemies & Mordecai's Greatness

OPENING PRAYER
READ: Esther 9:1-28 and 10:1-3

Now in the twelfth...

1) How did the Jews get relief from their enemies?_____
_____
_____

2) Why was Mordecai held in such high esteem in the kingdom?_____
_____

3) What prevented the Jews from annihilation? _____
_____

Explore God's World

MEMORY VERSES:

Genesis 17:5-6 No longer shall your name be called Abram, but your name shall be Abraham; for I have made you a father of many nations. I will make you exceedingly fruitful; and I will make nations of you, and kings shall come from you.

1ST PETER
Verse 1 identifies Apostle Peter as the author.
PURPOSE
1st Peter is a letter to the believers who had been dispersed throughout the ancient world and were under intense persecution. If anyone understood persecution it was Peter, who was beaten, threatened, punished, and jailed for preaching the Word of God. Peter, in great faith, knew what it took to live an obedient, victorious life without bitterness and losing hope. Knowledge of living hope in Jesus and following Christ's example is the message of this book.

For Your Information

FUN FACTS	THE SEVEN MOST DENSELY POPULATED US STATES	NETHERLANDS (HOLLAND)
1. North Korea uses a fax machine to send threats to South Korea. 2. The idea of using a parachute to fall gently to the ground was originated by Leonardo da Vinci. The first parachute was demonstrated by Louis-Sebastien Lenormand, of France, in 1783.	1) California 2) Texas 3) New York 4) Florida 5) Illinois 6) Pennsylvania 7) Ohio	...is in the continent of Europe. Amsterdam is the capital. Previously called Holland, the country has 20 national parks and hundreds of other nature reserves. Dutch cheese is the best cheese in the world, as agreed by 40 judges from 17 countries, who judged 2,500 cheeses in 2012 in USA.

GROUP DISCUSSION AND CLOSING PRAYER

"I am the wisest man alive, for I know one thing, and that is that I know nothing."

Socrates

Day 56 ~ Week in Review

TRUE OR FALSE — Circle T for true or F for false

T or F   The author of James is also thought to be the brother of Jesus Christ.

T or F   Namibia is known to be the world's oldest desert.

T or F   NZ is home to the world's smallest tuna and the rarest sea cucumber.

T or F   Nepal has close ties with both of its neighbors Pakistan and Tibet.

T or F   The name "Nauru" means "I go to the beach."

T or F   Netherlands has 20 national parks and hundreds of other nature reserves.

T or F   Peter was beaten, threatened, punished and jailed for preaching Jesus Christ.

T or F   Paul was very happy when he wrote 2nd Timothy.

T or F   The letter to Philemon is the shortest of Paul's writings.

T or F   The major agricultural products of Myanmar are wheat, cotton and corn.

FILL IN THE BLANKS

a. Nauru is the_____state in the _____Pacific and the third _____state by area in the world.

b. Namibia is_____as the "_____of_____."

c. Previously called_____, the Netherlands has 20_____parks and_____of other
   nature_____.

d. Titus is_____as one of the_____epistles, as are the two_____to Timothy.

e. Ostriches can_____ faster than _____, and the_____can roar like lion.

f. English,_____, and NZ_____Language are the official_____of_____.

g. Your _____, not your _____, will _____your altitude.

h. Myanmar is the_____40th_____country and the _____largest in _____Asia.

i. Phonophobia is the _____of loud sounds, _____or of one's_____voice.

j. In Nepal,_____is one of the_____places and the_____of Lord_____Buddha.

MEMORIZE AND WRITE

Genesis 17:5-6 _____

_____

_____

_____

MATCH THE FOLLOWING

_____ a. Philemon	1. Yaren
_____ b. Namibia	2. Uncertain
_____ c. Titus	3. Naypyidaw
_____ d. 2nd Timothy	4. Kathmandu
_____ e. Netherlands (Holland)	5. Wellington
_____ f. Nauru	6. Pastoral Epistles
_____ g. Nepal	7. Onesimus
_____ h. Myanmar (Burma)	8. Paul
_____ i. New Zealand (NZ)	9. Windhoek
_____ j. Hebrews	10. Amsterdam

LIST THE SEVEN MOST DENSELY POPULATED US STATES

1. _____ 2. _____

3. _____ 4. _____

5. _____ 6. _____

7. _____

ESTHER

In what ways can we know the truth that Esther was chosen, "For such a time as this"? Can you think of things that are happening in your life or in the lives of your family members that God might be using, "For such a time as this"?

_____

_____

_____

_____

_____

_____

_____

_____

Esther Reveals Haman's Plot Coloring Activity
*Note, you may make copies of this page to color if multiple family members in
the same household want to color the illustration.*

Day 57 ~ Job's Piety, Prosperity, & Perseverance

There was a man...

OPENING PRAYER
READ: Job 1:1-22 and 2:1-13

1) What kind of man was Job? _____
_____

2) Why did God allow for Job to lose his wealth, servants, and children? _____
_____

3) What advice did Job's wife and three friends give Job? _____
_____
_____

Explore God's World

MEMORY VERSES:
Genesis 17:20 And as for Ishmael, I have heard you. Behold, I have blessed him, and will make him fruitful, and will multiply him exceedingly. He shall beget twelve princes, and I will make him a great nation.

2ND PETER
Verse 1 states that the author was apostle Peter, whose authorship has been challenged more than any other book in the New Testament. However, the early church fathers found no credible reason to reject his authorship.

PURPOSE
Peter, alarmed that false teachers were beginning to infiltrate the churches, called on Christians to grow stronger in their faith so that they would not defect, but rather combat the spreading apostasy. He strongly stressed the authenticity of the Word of God and the sure return of the Lord Jesus.

For Your Information

FUN FACTS	THE TOP FIVE COUNTRIES WITH THE MOST CONTENTED PEOPLE	NICARAGUA
1. The Korean version of "LOL" is "KKK" which means "Hahaha." 2. Forensic scientists can determine a person's sex, age, and race just by examining a single strand of hair.	1) Norway 2) Denmark 3) Sweden 4) New Zealand 5) Australia	...is in the continent of North America. Managua is the capital. This country is known for having the only freshwater sharks and the biggest lake island in the world. The main language is Spanish, although native tribes speak Miskito, Sumo Rama, and English Creole.

GROUP DISCUSSION AND CLOSING PRAYER

"Your present circumstances don't determine where you can go; they merely determine where you start."

Nido Qubein

Day 58 ~ Eliphaz & Job's Dialogue

Even as I have...

OPENING PRAYER

READ: Job 4:8; 5:7; 7:16; 15:6 & 20; 16:2 &19; 22:5 & 21-23 & 23:3-4 as well as Bildad and Job's Dialogue: Job 8:3 & 5-6; 10:2; 18:2 & 5; 19:3 & 21; 25:4; & 27:5

1) According to Eliphaz why do bad things happen to people?_____
_____

2) What did Eliphaz say to Job in 5:7? _____
_____

3) In Job 18:5 what did Bildad say would happen to the wicked?_____
_____

Explore God's World

MEMORY VERSES:

Genesis 17:20 And as for Ishmael, I have heard you. Behold, I have blessed him, and will make him fruitful, and will multiply him exceedingly. He shall beget twelve princes, and I will make him a great nation.

1ST JOHN

1st, 2nd, and 3rd John are attributed to the Apostle John, who also wrote the Gospel of John. The content, style, and vocabulary of these three epistles addressed the same readers as the Gospel of John.

PURPOSE

The key purpose of 1st John is to set boundaries on the content of faith and to give believers assurance of their salvation through Jesus Christ. The epistle indicates that the believers were mixing the false teaching of "Gnosticism", a pagan philosophy, with their own faith. This godless belief, in which matter is evil, spirit is good, and knowledge or "gnosis" comes from man's rise from the mundane to the spiritual, led to two theories concerning the person of Christ: "Docetism", in which the human Jesus is regarded as a ghost, and "Cerinthianism", in which Jesus is a dual personality, both human and divine.

For Your Information

FUN FACTS	THE TOP FIVE COUNTRIES WITH THE MOST CONTENTED PEOPLE	NIGER
1. The King James Bible has inspired the lyrics of more pop songs than any other book. 2. A cruise ship named "The World" is the permanent home for its residents.	1) Norway 2) Denmark 3) Sweden 4) New Zealand 5) Australia	...is in the continent of Africa. Niamey is the capital. It is nicknamed "Frying Pan of the World", as it is one of the hottest countries in the world. Niger has the lowest "Human Development Index" on earth. Niger is the largest exporter of uranium.

GROUP DISCUSSION AND CLOSING PRAYER

"If you accept the expectations of others, especially negative ones, then you never will change the outcome."

Michael Jordan

Day 59 ~ Zophar & Job's Dialogue

OPENING PRAYER
READ: Job 11:11-14; 13:3-4; 20:5 and 21:7 as well as Elihu and Job's Dialogue: Job 33:12-13 and 36:11-13

For he knows...

1) In Job 11:11 of whom did Zophar say God takes notice? _____

2) In Job13:3 with whom did Job say he would like to argue his case? _____

3) In what different ways does God speak to people, according to Elihu in Job 33:12-13? _____

Explore God's World

MEMORY VERSES:

Genesis 17:20 And as for Ishmael, I have heard you. Behold, I have blessed him, and will make him fruitful, and will multiply him exceedingly. He shall beget twelve princes, and I will make him a great nation.

2ND JOHN
See authorship of 1 John.

PURPOSE
2nd John is an urgent plea to the readers that they show their love for God, and His son Jesus, by obeying the commandment to love each other and live their lives in obedience to the Scriptures. John also issued a strong warning for believers to be on the lookout for deceivers, who were going about saying that Christ had not actually risen in the flesh.

For Your Information

FUN FACTS	THE TOP FIVE COUNTRIES WITH THE MOST CONTENTED PEOPLE	NIGERIA
1. The terms "white meat" and "dark meat" originated during the Victoria era when people were too embarrassed to say 'leg' and "breast." 2. There is more real lemon juice in Lemon Pledge furniture polish than in Country Time Lemonade.	1) Norway 2) Denmark 3) Sweden 4) New Zealand 5) Australia	…is in the continent of Africa. Abuja is the capital. Nigeria has the 10th largest proven reserves of petroleum worldwide. The largest ethnic groups are the Hausa, Yoruba, Igbo, and Fulani. The number of languages is estimated to be 521.

GROUP DISCUSSION AND CLOSING PRAYER

"God always gives His best to those who leave the choice with Him."

Jim Elliot

Day 60 ~ Job's Reply & God's Sovereignty

OPENING PRAYER
READ: Job 40:3-24

Then Job answered...

1) What was Job's response to God? _____

_____

2) In verse 9, what can we learn about God? _____

_____

3) What did God say about the behemoth? _____

_____

_____

Explore God's World

MEMORY VERSES:

Genesis 17:20 And as for Ishmael, I have heard you. Behold, I have blessed him, and will make him fruitful, and will multiply him exceedingly. He shall beget twelve princes, and I will make him a great nation.

3RD JOHN
See authorship of 1 John.

PURPOSE
John's purpose in writing this third epistle is threefold. First, he writes to commend and encourage his beloved co-worker Gaius in his ministry of hospitality to those who were going from place to place to preach the Gospel of Christ. Second, he indirectly warns and condemns the behavior of Diotrephes, a dictatorial leader, who had taken over one of the rectly opposed to apostle Paul's teaching. Third, he commends the example of Demetrius, who was reported from all as having a good testimony.

For Your Information

FUN FACTS	THE TOP FIVE COUNTRIES WITH THE MOST CONTENTED PEOPLE	NORWAY
1. Nearly 4 million cats are eaten in China every year, as a delicacy. 2. According to the Wildlife Conservation Society, the perfume "Obsession for Men" attracts jaguars, pumas and other wildlife.	1) Norway 2) Denmark 3) Sweden 4) New Zealand 5) Australia	…is in the continent of Europe. Oslo is the capital. Norway, means "the northward route" It maintains embassies in 86 countries, while 60 countries maintain embassies in Oslo. The country has extensive reserves of petroleum, natural gas, minerals, lumber, seafood, fresh water, and hydropower.

GROUP DISCUSSION AND CLOSING PRAYER

"Live as if you were to die tomorrow. Learn as if you were to live forever."

Mahatma Gandhi

Day 61 ~ God's Sovereignty

OPENING PRAYER
READ: Job 41:1-34

Can you draw...

1) What did God say about the leviathan? _____
_____

2) To whom does everything under the heaven belong?_____
_____

3) What lesson can we learn in verses 31-32?_____
_____

Explore God's World

MEMORY VERSES:
Genesis 17:20 And as for Ishmael, I have heard you. Behold, I have blessed him, and will make him fruitful, and will multiply him exceedingly. He shall beget twelve princes, and I will make him a great nation.

JUDE
Jude 1 identifies the author as Jude, a brother of James. This likely refers to Jesus' half-brother Jude, as Jesus also had a half-brother named James (Matthew 13:55). Jude likely does not identify himself as a brother of Jesus out of humility and reverence for Christ.

PURPOSE
Jude is an important book for us today because it is written for the end times, when the church age, which began at the Day of Pentecost, ceases. Jude is the only biblical book given entirely to the future's great apostasy and the apostasy which had infiltrated the churches of Jude's time. Evil works are the evidence of apostasy, he writes. Because the saints were in danger of being mislead spiritually by the false teachers in the church, he admonished believers to "earnestly contend for the faith which was once delivered unto the saints" (Jude 3). Jude has vital application for the Christians of today.

For Your Information

FUN FACTS	THE TOP FIVE COUNTRIES WITH THE MOST CONTENTED PEOPLE	PAKISTAN
1."Taphephobia" is the fear of being buried alive. 2. Leonardo da Vinci made detailed sketches of the airplane, helicopter, parachute, submarine, armored car, and ballista rapid-fire guns.	1) Norway 2) Denmark 3) Sweden 4) New Zealand 5) Australia	...is in the continent of Asia; Islamabad is the capital. The country has four of the fourteen highest peaks in the world; K2 is the second highest mountain in the world, The Khewra salt mine is the second largest salt mine in the world. After Indonesia, Pakistan is the 2nd largest Islamic country.

GROUP DISCUSSION AND CLOSING PRAYER

"What great thing would you attempt if you knew you could not fail?"

Robert H. Schuller

Day 62 ~ Job's Repentance & Blessings

OPENING PRAYER
READ: Job 42:1-17

Now when the people...

1) Why was God angry with Job's three friends, but not with Job?_____
_____

2) How did the Lord bless Job again? _____
_____

3) What lesson can you learn from Job's life?_____
_____

Explore God's World

MEMORY VERSES:

Genesis 17:20 And as for Ishmael, I have heard you. Behold, I have blessed him, and will make him fruitful, and will multiply him exceedingly. He shall beget twelve princes, and I will make him a great nation.

REVELATION

Rev 1:1, 4, 9 and 22:8 specifically identify the author as the apostle John. The word revelation is from the Greek word "apokalupsis", which means "a disclosure or an unveiling."

PURPOSE

The Revelation of Jesus Christ was given to John to "show his servant what must soon take warning that the world, as we know it, will end and that God's judgment is certain. John is given a glimpse of heaven and all the glories awaiting those who remain faithful to Jesus Christ. Revelation foretells the great tribulation woes, the final fire reserved for unbelievers for eternity, the final doom for Satan and his angels, and the duties of all the angels and heavenly creatures. As an eyewitness to the unveiling of the punitive as well as the restoration of end times, John used language that has been an obstacle for readers for centuries; yet 1:7 reads, "Blessed is he that reads, and they that hear the words of this prophecy…" Today Revelation is more understandable because of the fulfillment of prophecies necessary before the end times and of the rampant evil in the world, and book pulls together all the prophecies of the Old Testament.

For Your Information

FUN FACTS	THE TOP FIVE COUNTRIES WITH THE MOST CONTENTED PEOPLE	OMAN
1. Durand Cup is associated with the game of Football. 2. According to gaming laws, casinos have to stock enough cash to cover chips on the "floor."	1) Norway 2) Denmark 3) Sweden 4) New Zealand 5) Australia	…is in the continent of Asia. Muscat is the capital. At least 12 different languages are native to Omani citizens. The future is uncertain because of its limited oil reserves, though they currently enjoy good living standards, the. The official religion is Ibadi Islam.

GROUP DISCUSSION AND CLOSING PRAYER

"It is not the body's posture, but the heart's attitude that counts when we pray."

Billy Graham

Day 63 ~ Week in Review

MEMORIZE AND WRITE

Genesis 17:20 _____

_____

_____

TRUE OR FALSE — Circle T for true or F for false

T or F   Jude is an important book for us today because it is written for the end times.

T or F   Norway means "the northward route".

T or F   The official religion in Oman is Wahabbi Islam.

T or F   John's beloved co-worker Gaius was instrumental in his ministry of hospitality.

T or F   Pakistan holds fourteen out of fourteen highest peaks in the world.

T or F   The number of languages estimated in Nigeria is 521.

T or F   Revelation is filled with mysteries about things to come.

T or F   Sudan and Saudi Arabia are the happy countries to live in.

T or F   The main language in Nicaragua is French, although native tribes speak Arabic and Hindi.

T or F   Niger has highest "Human Development Index" on earth

MATCH THE FOLLOWING

_____ a. Docetism   1. Abuja

_____ b. Norway   2. Making Jesus a dual personality

_____ c. Jude   3. Niamey

_____ d. Oman   4. Oslo

_____ e. Nicaragua   5. The human Jesus as a ghost

_____ f. Cerinthianism   6. Islamabad

_____ g. Revelation   7. Muscat

_____ h. Niger   8. Managua

_____ i. Pakistan   9. A brother of James

_____ j. Nigeria   10. A disclosure, an unveiling

LIST THE TOP FIVE COUNTRIES WITH THE MOST CONTENTED PEOPLE

1. _____   2. _____

3. _____   4. _____

5. _____

FILL IN THE BLANKS

a. Nigeria's largest _____ groups are the _____ , Yoruba, _____ and _____ Fulani.

b. Taphephobia is the _____ of being _____ _____ .

c. Jude has vital _____ for the _____ of today.

d. After Indonesia, _____ is the 2nd _____ Islamic _____ .

e. Norway, means "the _____ route" (the "way _____ " or the " _____ ").

f. Nicaragua is _____ for the only _____ sharks and the biggest lake _____ in the world.

g. Revelation is from the _____ word _____ which means, " _____ , an _____ ."

h. At least 12 different _____ are _____ to Omani citizens.

i. Every _____ , nearly 4 _____ cats are eaten in _____ as a delicacy.

j. Niger is one of the _____ countries in the _____ and is nicknamed " _____ Pan of the World."

k. The terms " _____ _____ " and "dark meat" _____ during the _____ era when people were too _____ to say 'leg" and "breast."

JOB

Why do you believe that God pointed out Job to Satan when Satan came before God's throne? Do you believe you are living life in such faithfulness to God that He would see in you the qualities that He saw in Job? What can you do to be a testimony in times of great trouble?

_____

_____

_____

_____

_____

_____

_____

_____

_____

_____

Job Confronted by His Friends Coloring Activity

Note, you may make copies of this page to color if multiple family members in the same household want to color the illustration.

Day 64 ~ What Are Psalms

OPENING PRAYER
READ: Psalm 23; Also, read the "Overview of Psalms" below before answering the questions.

The Lord is...

1) What is meaning of the word "Psalm"? How many different types are there?_____

_____

2) To whom are the Psalms attributed? _____

_____

3) How many Psalms are in the Bible? Which one is the shortest? The longest?_____

_____

Explore God's World

MEMORY VERSES:

Genesis 1:1-2 In the beginning God created the heavens and the earth. The earth was without form, and void; and darkness was on the face of the deep. And the Spirit of God was hovering over the face of the waters.

OVERVIEW OF PSALMS

The Hebrew title of the book, also called the Psalter, translates to "praises". The word "psalm" comes from the Greek psalmoi, meaning "songs." Originally, these 150 poems were meant to be sung and were used in ancient Jewish worship services accompanied by lyres, flutes, horns, and cymbals. King David established a 4,000 piece orchestra to play during worship (1st Chronicles 23:5).

There are many different **types of psalms**, the two main types being **laments** (prayers in times of need or sorrow) and **songs of praise** (worship in times of joy). However, there are also: **songs of thanksgiving** (for specific instances when God answered prayer), **wisdom psalms** (designed for teaching), **royal psalms** (written for the king), **confessions of trust** (used when facing a specific trial), **temple entry liturgies** (sung together before entering the temple), and **pilgrim songs** (sung together on a pilgrimage).

The authors and the number of Psalms attributed to them are: David-73; Asaph-12; Sons of Korah-9; Solomon-2; Heman-1; Ethan-1; Moses-1; and anonymous-51.

For Your Information

FUN FACTS	THE SEVEN HOTTEST COUNTRIES OF THE WORLD	PALAU
1. Qatar is the only country which starts with letter Q. 2. Alexander Graham Bell invented the telephone with Thomas Watson in 1876.	1) Libya 2) Saudi Arabia 3) Iraq 4) Algeria 5) Iran 6) Oman 7) Sudan	...is in the continent of Australia (Oceanic). Melekeok is the capital. The country is vulnerable to earthquakes, volcanic activity, and tropical storms. Saltwater crocodiles are also "residents." Its economy consists primarily of tourism, subsistence agriculture, and fishing.

GROUP DISCUSSION AND CLOSING PRAYER

"Prayer is the link that connects us with God."

A.B. Simpson

Day 65 ~ Psalms of Laments

To You I will cry...

1) What Did David believe would happen if the Lord did not answer his prayer?_____
_____

2) How did David want the Lord to deal with the wicked? _____
_____

3) What did David expect the Lord to do for His people? _____
_____
_____

Explore God's World

MEMORY VERSES:

Genesis 1:1-2 In the beginning God created the heavens and the earth. The earth was without form, and void; and darkness was on the face of the deep. And the Spirit of God was hovering over the face of the waters.

SYNOPSIS OF GENESIS
The book was written by Moses about 1450-1410 B.C. Key personalities include Adam, Eve, Noah, Abraham, Sarah, Isaac, Rebekah, Jacob, and Joseph. The first book of the Law, and also the first book of the entire Bible, was written to record God's creation of the world and to demonstrate His love for all that He created. Genesis, literally meaning "In the beginning", explains the actual events of one of the most debated subjects of our current day-the origin of life. Genesis describes the Lord God as infinite and all-powerful, Word. He essentially creates material matter out of nonmaterial nothing.

For Your Information

FUN FACTS	THE SEVEN HOTTEST COUNTRIES OF THE WORLD	PALESTINE
1. Leonardo Da Vinci was the first to explain why the sky is blue. 2. Army ants are used as natural sutures. Because the ants' jaws are so powerful that indigenous Americans used to staple their wounds by forcing ants to bite them and then break off the bodies.	1) Libya 2) Saudi Arabia 3) Iraq 4) Algeria 5) Iran 6) Oman 7) Sudan	...is in the continent of Africa; Ramallah is the capital. Palestine has one of the world's oldest Churches, the Church of Nativity, which is identified as the place of Jesus Christ's birth and is considered to be sacred by Christians and Muslims alike. Christmas is celebrated three times a year in the Palestinian territories because Catholics and Protestants celebrate on December 25. Most Orthodox Churches, including the Greek Orthodox, Ethiopian, Russian Orthodox, Coptic, and Syrian celebrate Christmas on January 7, because of the Gregorian calendar in 1576. While the Armenian Orthodox Church in Jerusalem celebrates Christmas on January 19, due to another calendar change.

GROUP DISCUSSION AND CLOSING PRAYER
"To deny people their human rights is to challenge their very humanity."
Nelson Mandela

Day 66 ~ Psalms–Praises

OPENING PRAYER
READ: Psalm 19 and 33

The heavens declare...

1) What do the heavens and the skies say to us in Psalm 19? _____

_____

2) How does the sun affect the earth according to Psalm 19? _____

_____

3) How has the Lord demonstrated His creativity in Psalm 33? _____

_____

_____

Explore God's World

MEMORY VERSES:
  Genesis 1:1-2 In the beginning
  God created the heavens and
  the earth. The earth was without
  form, and void; and darkness was
  on the face of the deep. And the
  Spirit of God was hovering over
  the face of the waters.

SYNOPSIS OF EXODUS
The book consists mainly of two genres narrative history
and law, was written by Moses about 1450-1410 B.C. The
key personalities include Moses, Miriam, Pharaoh, Pharaoh's
daughter, Aaron, and Joshua. Written to record the events of
Israel's deliverance from slavery in Egypt, Exodus describes
the events in chronological order, and also lists the laws that
God gave to the Israelites in order to guide them in their
relationship with Him.

For Your Information

FUN FACTS	THE SEVEN HOTTEST COUNTRIES OF THE WORLD	PANAMA
1. John F. Kennedy was buried without his brain after it was lost during the autopsy. 2. Technically the almond is not a nut. It is actually the pit of a fruit related to peaches, plums, and apricots.	1) Libya 2) Saudi Arabia 3) Iraq 4) Algeria 5) Iran 6) Oman 7) Sudan	...is in the continent of North America. Panama City is the capital. Coastlines on both the North Pacific Ocean and the Caribbean Sea define Panama's borders. One can see both the Atlantic and the Pacific oceans when standing on the 11,450-foot-high summit of Volcán Barú.

GROUP DISCUSSION AND CLOSING PRAYER

"Faith must have adequate evidence, else it is mere superstition."

A.A. Hodge

JOURNEY *to my* FAITH *Family Devotional Series* — VOLUME 2

Day 67 ~ Psalms–Thanksgiving

OPENING PRAYER
READ: Psalm 100 and 124

Make a joyful...

1) How are we to come into His presence? _____

_____

2) How would Israel have been treated if God were not on her side? _____

_____

3) In Psalm 124 what did David realize about his abilities in comparison to the Lord's power? _____

_____

_____

Explore God's World

MEMORY VERSES:

Genesis 1:1-2 In the beginning God created the heavens and the earth. The earth was without form, and void; and darkness was on the face of the deep. And the Spirit of God was hovering over the face of the waters.

SYNOPSIS OF LEVITICUS

The book is composed of narrative history and law, was written by Moses about 1445-1444 B.C. where the setting mainly appears to take place at Mt. Sinai. Moses urged the Israelites to understand the infinite holiness of God, who desired them to act in a holy manner toward Himself. Through Moses, God gave the Israelites instructions in holy living, especially to the Levitical priests, by giving them details in observing specific celebrations, ceremonies, and various offerings. The word "holy" is mentioned more times in Leviticus than in any other book in the Bible.

For Your Information

FUN FACTS	THE SEVEN HOTTEST COUNTRIES OF THE WORLD	PAPUA NEW GUINEA
1. Flight numbers are often taken out of use after a crash or a serious incident. 2. A study conducted by the University of Hawaii at Manoa revealed that shorter men live longer lives than tall men.	1) Libya 2) Saudi Arabia 3) Iraq 4) Algeria 5) Iran 6) Oman 7) Sudan	...is in the continent of Australia (Oceanic). Port Moresby is the capital. A team of scientists found more than 40 previously unidentified species in the crater of Mount Bosavi. They found 16 types of frogs, fish, a bat, and a giant rat, which may turn out to be the biggest in the world. The country official languages are English, Tok Pisin, and Hiri Motu. Rugby is the national sport of the Papua New Guinea.

GROUP DISCUSSION AND CLOSING PRAYER

"A man must be big enough to admit his mistakes, smart enough to profit from them, and strong enough to correct them."

John C. Maxwell

Day 68 ~ Psalms–Confession

OPENING PRAYER
READ: Psalm 51

Have mercy on...

1) What was the writer's attitude toward his sin? _____
_____

2) What does the author of this Psalm desire? _____
_____

3) How does the prayer for Jerusalem serve as a fitting conclusion for this Psalm?_____
_____
_____

Explore God's World

MEMORY VERSES:
Genesis 1:1-2 In the beginning God created the heavens and the earth. The earth was without form, and void; and darkness was on the face of the deep. And the Spirit of God was hovering over the face of the waters.

SYNOPSIS OF NUMBERS
The book is largely narrative history as its genre, was written by Moses about 1450-1410 B.C. Key personalities include Moses, Aaron, Miriam, Joshua, Caleb, Eleazar, Korah, and Balaam. Numbers tells the history of how Israel prepared to enter the promise land but sinned and was punished. The book describes two population censuses Moses took. Hence, the name Numbers.

For Your Information

FUN FACTS	THE SEVEN HOTTEST COUNTRIES OF THE WORLD	PARAGUAY
1. The volcanic rock known as "pumice" is the only rock that can float in water. 2. Footprints and tire tracks left behind by astronauts on the moon will stay there forever as there is no wind to blow them away.	1) Libya 2) Saudi Arabia 3) Iraq 4) Algeria 5) Iran 6) Oman 7) Sudan	...is in the continent of South America. Asuncion is the capital. Guaraní and Spanish are the official languages. Paraguay has compulsory military service for all 18-year-old males. Roman Catholicism is the dominant religion. Football is the most popular sports.

GROUP DISCUSSION AND CLOSING PRAYER

"There has never been a spiritual awakening in any country or locality that did not begin in united prayer."

A.T. Pierson

Day 69 ~ Psalms–Other

OPENING PRAYER
READ: Psalm 2 and 101

Why do the nations...

1) What did the rulers of the world want to accomplish according to Psalm 2?_____
_____

2) What promises did David make to the Lord according to Psalm 101?_____
_____

3) What was David's attitude toward the wicked in Psalm 101?_____
_____
_____

Explore God's World

MEMORY VERSES:

Genesis 1:1-2 In the beginning God created the heavens and the earth. The earth was without form, and void; and darkness was on the face of the deep. And the Spirit of God was hovering over the face of the waters.

SYNOPSIS OF DEUTERONOMY

The genre of the book is not much different from that of Exodus, mainly, narrative history and Law, although there is a Song from Moses just after he commissions Joshua. This song describes the history that the Israelites had experienced. Deuteronomy, written approximately1407-1406 B.C., sums up Moses' review to the Israelites of what God had done for them and of what God expected of them. The key personalities are Moses and Joshua. The name literally means "Second Law," as Moses gives "the Law" for the second time.

For Your Information

FUN FACTS	THE SEVEN HOTTEST COUNTRIES OF THE WORLD	PERU
1. English has only one word for "love" while Sanskrit has 96. 2. "Strengths" is the longest world in the English language with only one vowel.	1) Libya 2) Saudi Arabia 3) Iraq 4) Algeria 5) Iran 6) Oman 7) Sudan	...is in the continent of South America. Lima is the capital. The country is rich in resources of copper, silver and gold and is well known for its pottery, textiles, traditional cooking, paintings, and sculptures. Peru's major trade partners are the US, China, Brazil and Chile. The country is bordered in the north by Ecuador and Colombia, in the east by Brazil, in the southeast by Bolivia, in the south by Chile, and in the west by the Pacific Ocean.

GROUP DISCUSSION AND CLOSING PRAYER

"Love and compassion are necessities, not luxuries. Without them humanity cannot survive."

Dalai Lama

Day 70 ~ Week in Review

MATCH THE FOLLOWING

_____ a. Panama	1. History and Laws
_____ b. Papua New Guinea	2. Melekeok
_____ c. Peru	3. In the Beginning
_____ d. Palestine	4. Asuncion
_____ e. Numbers	5. Second Law
_____ f. Palau	6. Panama City
_____ g. Exodus	7. Population censuses
_____ h. Deuteronomy	8. Lima
_____ i. Paraguay	9. Port Moresby
_____ j. Genesis	10. Ramallah

TRUE OR FALSE — Circle T for true or F for false

T or F   Equatorial Guinea is the only Africa country whose official language is Spanish.

T or F   Asmara is the capital of Eritrea and listed in the continent of Asia.

T or F   2nd Timothy has only 4 chapters.

T or F   Skating was invented by Ado Kosh.

T or F   Queen Sheba was from Ethiopia.

T or F   Fiji consists of 349 islands.

T or F   The Harbor of Rio de Janerio is in Brazil.

T or F   The Taj Mahal is in Pakistan.

T or F   Finland has no fresh water lakes.

T or F   1st Peter's theme is Christian Living.

MEMORIZE AND WRITE

Genesis 1:1-2 _____

_____

_____

_____

LIST THE SEVEN HOTTEST COUNTRIES OF THE WORLD

1. _____ 2. _____

3. _____ 4. _____

5. _____ 6. _____

7. _____

FILL IN THE BLANKS

a. Exodus consists mainly of _____ genres, narrative _____ and _____.

b. Christmas is celebrated _____ times a _____ in the Palestinian _____.

c. The word "_____" is mentioned in Leviticus more _____, than any other book in the

   _____.

d. The word "psalm" _____ from the Greek _____, meaning "_____."

e. Paraguay has _____ military service for all _____-year-old _____.

f. Palau is _____ to earthquakes, _____ activity, and _____ storms.

g. Numbers tells the _____ of how _____ prepared to enter the _____ land but sinned and was

   _____.

h. What are the _____ of Psalms attributed to them: _____-73; Asaph-12; Sons of _____ - 9;
   _____-2; Heman _____ ; Ethan _____; Moses-1; and _____-51.

i. Genesis, include _____, Eve, Noah, _____, Sarah, Isaac, _____, Jacob,
   and _____.

j. In Panama one can _____ both the _____ and the Pacific Oceans when _____ on
   the 11,450- _____-_____ summit of Volcán _____.

HOW DOES GOD DEAL WITH PEOPLE?

What are some ways that God deals with the wicked, especially in this "age of grace"? What does God expect us, as His people, to do?

_____

_____

_____

_____

_____

_____

Bible Word Search

```
S M L A S P X F P R F T A S P
P I H M G B C I I I H X T G I
P C G W V I H X M A L R L N S
S N O I S S E F N O C G A O O
Z N Q U R G A K D C D G R S L
Y P M O I B S K M A P S J I O
Z T W G I G O A S E V W I A M
R R I L I R J U E V A I W W O
X D I V A T R U S T S F D V N
B T I H I Y L N I N A M E H S
Y N Q G I T H C A E P B B I E
G C R F A V A M R H H G S N S
I X I F Y L B E P C T E K M O
J Z J T H D F I R L P E N Q M
L A M E N T S C W C B J H R V
```

ABILITY	ASAPH	CONFESSIONS
CREATIVITY	DAVID	ETHAN
HEMAN	KORAH	LAMENTS
MOSES	MUSIC	PILGRIM
PRAISES	PSALMS	SOLOMON
SONGS	THANKSGIVING	TRUST
WISDOM	WORSHIP	

Day 71 ~ The Fear of the Lord

OPENING PRAYER
READ: Proverbs 1:1-33

The proverbs of Solomon...

1) What is the result of not accepting wisdom? _____
_____

2) How should a person treat those in need? _____
_____

3) What are the benefits of following wisdom? _____
_____

Explore God's World

MEMORY VERSES:
2nd Timothy 4:7-8 I have fought the good fight, I have finished the race, I have kept the faith. Finally, there is laid up for me the crown of righteousness, which the Lord, the righteous Judge, will give to me on that Day, and not to me only, but also to all who have loved His appearing.

SYNOPSIS OF JOSHUA
The book is narrative history authored by Joshua, the leader of the Israelites, circa 1405-1383 B.C. The key personalities are Joshua, Rahab, Achan, Phinehas, and Eleazar. It records the Israelites' conquest of the Promised Land, as well as the Living God rewarding the Israelites' obedience. As the leader of the nation after Moses, Joshua demonstrates his faith in God by following the Almighty's instructions. Joshua truly was "strong and courageous"(1:7).

For Your Information

FUN FACTS	THE SEVEN COLDEST COUNTRIES OF THE WORLD	PHILIPPINES
1. Pope Francis claims that pets and animals can go to heaven. 2. Punjab is the land of five rivers in North West India and North East Pakistan.	1) Russia 2) Canada 3) Mongolia 4) Finland 5) Iceland 6) Kazakhstan 7) Sweden	...is in the continent of Asia. Manila is the capital. The Philippines is one of the largest island groups in the world with 7,107 islands, which include the fantastic Chocolate Hills in Bohol, the Rice Terraces in Banaue, and the incredible Archipelago of El Nido. People can climb the 37 volcanoes, or see the world's smallest volcano of Taal.

GROUP DISCUSSION AND CLOSING PRAYER

"Prayer is a virtue that prevaileth against all temptations.'"
Bernard of Clairvaux

Day 72 ~ Walk with Humility

OPENING PRAYER
READ: Proverbs 3:1-35

My son, do not forget...

1) What lesson can we learn from verses 5 and 6?_____
_____

2) What is better than gold and silver? _____
_____

3) What happens to the house of the wicked and of the just man? _____
_____
_____

Explore God's World

MEMORY VERSES:

2nd Timothy 4:7-8 I have fought the good fight, I have finished the race, I have kept the faith. Finally, there is laid up for me the crown of righteousness, which the Lord, the righteous Judge, will give to me on that Day, and not to me only, but also to all who have loved His appearing.

SYNOPSIS OF JUDGES

The book of Judges includes several interesting genres; poetry, riddles, and narrative history. Its author is anonymous but is usually assumed to be Samuel, the prophet. He wrote the book about 1086-1004 B.C. The book of Judges relates that God was faithful to Israel, but certainly punished their sin of disobedience; therefore, each person must remain loyal and devoted to Him. This book records the history of the generations of Israelites during the period of the Judges, who ruled Israel after Joshua's death. It covers the consequences of obedience and disobedience, faithfulness and unfaithfulness, captivity and oppression, repentance, deliverance, and obedience once again. It deals with the results of these courses of action and the consequences that follow. It also shows that the results are similar to what we have seen in the previous books.

For Your Information

FUN FACTS	THE SEVEN COLDEST COUNTRIES OF THE WORLD	PORTUGAL
1. The place where military personnel socialize and eat is called the mess hall. 2. Before the mid-19th century, dentures were commonly made with teeth pulled from the mouths of dead soldiers.	1) Russia 2) Canada 3) Mongolia 4) Finland 5) Iceland 6) Kazakhstan 7) Sweden	...is in the continent of Europe. Lisbon is the capital. The country is famous for its delicious pastries and espresso coffee. Portugal has had the same defined borders since 1139, making it the oldest nation-state in Europe. Football is the most popular sport.

GROUP DISCUSSION AND CLOSING PRAYER

"We do not learn; and what we call learning is only a process of recollection."

Plato

Day 73 ~ Parent's Instructions

The proverbs of Solomon...

1) How does Solomon describe the wicked person?_____

_____

2) What are the characteristics of the righteous man?_____

_____

3) What do vinegar and smoke symbolize in verse 26?_____

_____

_____

Explore God's World

MEMORY VERSES:

2nd Timothy 4:7-8 I have fought the good fight, I have finished the race, I have kept the faith. Finally, there is laid up for me the crown of righteousness, which the Lord, the righteous Judge, will give to me on that Day, and not to me only, but also to all who have loved His appearing.

SYNOPSIS OF RUTH

The book is the narrative of a love story, yet also has some important genealogy. The timeline of this book is intertwined during the period of the Judges. The author was anonymous, but some believe it was perhaps written by Samuel the prophet; however, it is unlikely that he was alive when this book was written (about 1046-1035 B.C.). Key personalities include Ruth, Naomi, and Boaz. The book of Ruth, which demonstrates God's love and faithfulness, is a contrast to the book of Judges actions and consequences: what happens when God's people faithfully follow His covenant (Ruth); and what happens when the nation did not obediently follow the covenant of God (Judges).

For Your Information

FUN FACTS

1. Holding hands with someone you love can alleviate physical pain as well as stress and fear.
2. The electric iron was invented in 1882 by Henry W. Seeley. His iron weighed almost 15 pounds and took a long time to warm up.

THE SEVEN COLDEST COUNTRIES OF THE WORLD

1) Russia 2) Canada
3) Mongolia 4) Finland
5) Iceland 6) Kazakhstan
7) Sweden

POLAND

…is in the continent of Europe. Warsaw is the capital. Poland is famous for being the home of Pope John Paul II. The Polish are well educated with 90% of its youth completing secondary education and 50% having an academic degree. The Zloty is the Polish currency and the most popular sports are football and volleyball.

GROUP DISCUSSION AND CLOSING PRAYER

"The greatest day in your life and mine is when we take total responsibility for our attitudes. That's the day we truly grow up."

John C. Maxwell

Day 74 ~ God's Timing

OPENING PRAYER
READ: Ecclesiastes 3:1-18

To everything there is...

1) What lessons can we learn from verses 1-8? _____
_____

2) Whom will God bring to judgment? _____
_____

3) Why did the preacher say "all is vanity"? _____
_____

Explore God's World

MEMORY VERSES:
2nd Timothy 4:7-8 I have fought the good fight, I have finished the race, I have kept the faith. Finally, there is laid up for me the crown of righteousness, which the Lord, the righteous Judge, will give to me on that Day, and not to me only, but also to all who have loved His appearing.

SYNOPSIS OF 1ST SAMUEL
1st Samuel, is a narrative history and includes a great deal of drama. It was written by the last of the judges, Samuel, for whom the book is named. It was written about 930 B.C. Key personalities include Eli, Hannah, Samuel, Saul, Jonathan, and David. The book traces the history of the Israelites' first monarchy, which resulted in the nation, with exception of a few individuals, blatantly neglecting and abandoning God.

For Your Information

FUN FACTS	THE SEVEN COLDEST COUNTRIES OF THE WORLD	QATAR
1. Younger beavers stay with their parents for the first two years of their lives before going out on their own. 2. Astronauts can grow up to two inches while in space because of the lack of pressure put on the spine.	1) Russia 2) Canada 3) Mongolia 4) Finland 5) Iceland 6) Kazakhstan 7) Sweden	...is in the continent of Asia. Doha is the capital. Qatar has the world's 3rd largest natural gas and oil reserves in excess. The legal system is a mixture of civil law and Islamic law (Sharia law). Qatar has one land border. The country borders Saudi Arabia to the south. Football is the most popular sport.

GROUP DISCUSSION AND CLOSING PRAYER

"We cannot change our past. We cannot change the fact that people act in a certain way. We cannot change the inevitable. The only thing we can do is play on the one string we have, and that is our attitude"

Charles R. Swindoll

Day 75 ~ Trusting in God

OPENING PRAYER
READ: Ecclesiastes 5:1-20

Walk prudently when...

1) How should a person go to the house of God?_____
_____

2) What does Solomon say about vows made to God? _____
_____

3) What happens to the person who has wealth and possessions in verses 19 and 20?_____
_____
_____

Explore God's World

MEMORY VERSES:

2nd Timothy 4:7-8 I have fought the good fight, I have finished the race, I have kept the faith. Finally, there is laid up for me the crown of righteousness, which the Lord, the righteous Judge, will give to me on that Day, and not to me only, but also to all who have loved His appearing.

SYNOPSIS OF 2ND SAMUEL
The book of 2nd Samuel is a narrative history of the reign of David who becomes the King of Israel; the final chapters include two psalms of praise. Its authors are probably the prophets Nathan and Gad, who wrote it at about 930 B.C The key personalities are David, Joab, Bathsheba, Nathan, and Absalom. Approximately half of the book tells of King David's success and the other half shows his failures; yet David's accomplishments, through his submission to God, demonstrate effective leadership.

For Your Information

FUN FACTS	THE SEVEN COLDEST COUNTRIES OF THE WORLD	ROMANIA
1. The song "Jingle Bells" was written for Thanksgiving. 2. If you counted 24 hours a day, it would take 31,688 years to reach a "trillion."	1) Russia 2) Canada 3) Mongolia 4) Finland 5) Iceland 6) Kazakhstan 7) Sweden	...is in the continent of Europe. Bucharest is the capital. The name Romania derives from the Latin romanus, meaning "Citizen of Rome." The country has the richest gold resources in Europe. The Gold Museum in Brad is the only one of its kind in Europe.

GROUP DISCUSSION AND CLOSING PRAYER

"Fasting is abstaining from anything that hinders prayer."

Andrew Bonar

Day 76 ~ Conclusion of Life

OPENING PRAYER

READ: Ecclesiastes 11:1-10 and 12:1-14

Cast your bread...

1) What advice does Solomon have for the young? _____
_____

2) Why does Solomon tell his reader to fear God and keep His commandments? _____
_____

3) What is the whole duty of man? _____
_____
_____

Explore God's World

MEMORY VERSES:

2nd Timothy 4:7-8 I have fought the good fight, I have finished the race, I have kept the faith. Finally, there is laid up for me the crown of righteousness, which the Lord, the righteous Judge, will give to me on that Day, and not to me only, but also to all who have loved His appearing.

SYNOPSIS OF 1ST KINGS

The book of 1st Kings is narrative history and prophecy. The author is anonymous; however, some suggest it may be the prophet Jeremiah. It was written about 560-538 B.C. The key personalities are David, Solomon, Rehoboam, Jeroboam, Elijah, Ahab, and Jezebel. 1st Kings contrasts those who obeyed and disobeyed God throughout the ruling kings of Israel and Judah. The book describes the rule of Solomon as the last king of the United Kingdom of Israel, and then the split of the kingdom after his death. A great prayer to the Lord is recorded in chapter 8. The writer recounts the events of the Northern and Southern Kingdoms after the division. The Northern Kingdom retained the name Israel and the Southern Kingdom was known as Judah and was comprised of the tribes of Judah and Benjamin.

For Your Information

FUN FACTS	THE SEVEN COLDEST COUNTRIES OF THE WORLD	RUSSIA
1. It takes an interaction of 72 muscles to produce audible human speech. 2. The telephone (meaning "far sound") is the most widely used telecommunications device. It was invented in 1876 by Alexander Graham Bell (with Thomas Watson).	1) Russia 2) Canada 3) Mongolia 4) Finland 5) Iceland 6) Kazakhstan 7) Sweden	...is in the continent of Asia. Moscow is the capital. The world's largest country by area, Russia is the most powerful country in the Soviet Union. The Trans-Siberian Railway is the longest railway in the world, which crosses nearly all of Russia.

GROUP DISCUSSION AND CLOSING PRAYER

"Prayer is not monologue, but dialogue. God's voice, in response to mine, is its most essential part."

Andrew Murray

Day 77 ~ Week in Review

MEMORIZE AND WRITE

2nd Timothy 4:7-8_____

_____

_____

TRUE OR FALSE — Circle T for true or F for false

T or F   Ruth was written by Naomi and Boaz.

T or F   John Paul II was a Roman citizen.

T or F   Portugal is famous for pizza and spices cuisine.

T or F   1st Samuel was written to show how Samuel became the king of Israel.

T or F   In Joshua the key personalities are Rahab, Achan, Phinehas, and Eleazar.

T or F   Russia is the world's largest country by area.

T or F   The Philippines has 37 volcanoes that adventurers can climb and has the world's smallest volcano, Taal.

T or F   The book of Judges was written by Joshua and Moses.

T or F   Bucharest is the capital of Belgium and listed in the continent of Russia.

T or F   The legal system in Qatar is a mixture of civil law and European law.

MATCH THE FOLLOWING

_____ a. Qatar   1. Strong and Courageous

_____ b. Portugal   2. The Last Judge

_____ c. Poland   3. Manila

_____ d. Ruth   4. Bucharest

_____ e. 1st Samuel   5. History and Prophecy

_____ f. Joshua   6. Warsaw

_____ g. 1st Kings   7. Doha

_____ h. Philippines   8. Naomi and Boaz

_____ i. Russia   9. Moscow

_____ j. Romania   10. Lisbon

FILL IN THE BLANKS

a. Poland is _____ for being the home of _____ John _____ II.

b. Ruth is the _____ of a love _____ , yet also has _____ important _____.

c. Qatar has the world's 3rd _____ and _____ reserves in _____.

d. The Philippines is one of the _____ island groups in the _____ with _____ islands.

e. Romania _____ from the Latin _____ , meaning " _____ of _____ ".

f. The Trans-_____ Railway is the _____ longest railway which _____ nearly all of Russia.

g. Judges relates that _____ was faithful to Israel, but certainly _____ their sin of _____.

h. 2nd Samuel tells of King _____ success and the other _____ shows his _____.

i. Joshua _____ his faith in _____ by following the Almighty's _____.

j. Portugal has had the same _____ borders since _____ , making it the _____ nation-state in Europe.

WRITE THE SEVEN COLDEST COUNTRIES OF THE WORLD

1. _____   2. _____

3. _____   4. _____

5. _____   6. _____

7. _____

GODLY CHARACTERISTICS

List at least five Godly characteristics along with a way that each of you can demonstrate that quality in your own life.

_____

_____

_____

_____

_____

_____

_____

_____

The Wisdom of Solomon Coloring Activity
*Note, you may make copies of this page to color if multiple family members in
the same household want to color the illustration.*

Day 78 ~ Isaiah's Calling

OPENING PRAYER
READ: Isaiah 6:1-13

In the year...

1) When was Isaiah granted the vision of the Lord?_____
_____

2) How did Isaiah see himself once he had been exposed to God's glory?_____
_____

3) How did Isaiah respond to the Lord's call?_____
_____

Explore God's World

MEMORY VERSES:

Matthew 5:13-14 "You are the salt of the earth; but if the salt loses its flavor, how shall it be seasoned? It is then good for nothing but to be thrown out and trampled underfoot by men. You are the light of the world. A city that is set on a hill cannot be hidden."

SYNOPSIS OF 2ND KINGS

The book, written about 560-538 B.C., is narrative history and prophecy concerning the affairs of the divided kingdoms. The author is anonymous; however, some suggest the it may be the prophet Jeremiah. Key personalities include Elijah, Elisha, the woman from Shunem, Naaman, Jezebel, Jehu, Joash, Hezekiah, Sennacherib, Isaiah, Manasseh, Josiah, Jehoiakim, Zedekiah, and Nebuchadnezzar. The book reminds those who obey God, of His blessings, and those who refuse to obey and make Him ultimate ruler of their lives, of their fate. In this book all the kings of the northern kingdom and many of the kings in the southern kingdom lead the people far from the Lord and are lost in the onerous confusion of their sins. In an attempt to bring His people back to worshiping Him, God performed amazing miracles through His prophets, who continued to herald His message of the only hope for this still chosen nation.

For Your Information

FUN FACTS	THE SEVEN COUNTRIES WITH THE MOST SUICIDES	RWANDA
1. Alfred Bernard Nobel invented many powerful and relatively safe explosives and explosive devices. He left much of his fortune to award prizes (the Nobel prizes) each year to people who made advancements in physics, chemistry, physiology/medicine, literature, and world peace.	1) Lithuania 2) Russia 3) Belarus 4) Latvia 5) Estonia 6) Hungary 7) Slovenia	...is in the continent of Africa. Kigali is the capital. Christianity is the largest religion. The principal language is Kinyarwanda, with French and English as official languages. Coffee and tea are the major cash crops for export.

GROUP DISCUSSION AND CLOSING PRAYER

"Challenge yourself with something you know you could never do, and what you'll find is that you can overcome anything."

Anonymous

Day 79 ~ The Sign of The Birth of Immanuel

OPENING PRAYER
READ: Isaiah 7:10-25

Moreover the Lord...

1) What sign did God give King Ahaz? _____
_____

2) What is so important in verse 14? _____
_____

3) What was the prophecy concerning Immanuel?_____
_____

Explore God's World

MEMORY VERSES:

Matthew 5:13-14 "You are the salt of the earth; but if the salt loses its flavor, how shall it be seasoned? It is then good for nothing but to be thrown out and trampled underfoot by men. You are the light of the world. A city that is set on a hill cannot be hidden."

SYNOPSIS OF 1ST CHRONICLES
The book is narrative history and genealogies. The author appears to be the prophet Ezra, who wrote it circa 430 B.C. Events from 1000 to 960 B.C. are covered. Key personalities are King David and Solomon. This book parallels some of 2nd Samuel and therefore describes similar events. Written after the exile, 1st Chronicles relates the encouragement given to the remnant that came out of the Babylonian captivity. Listed in the first nine chapters, the ancestry of the nation (but not chronologically) was an important reminder to the returning exiles of their connection to the founding fathers.

For Your Information

FUN FACTS	THE SEVEN COUNTRIES WITH THE MOST SUICIDES	SAINT KITTS AND NEVIS
1. Every 90 seconds, one woman dies from a pregnancy or childbirth complication. 2. During pregnancy, some pregnant women crave nonfood items such as paper, clay, chalk, etc. It is an eating disorder called "Pica."	1) Lithuania 2) Russia 3) Belarus 4) Latvia 5) Estonia 6) Hungary 7) Slovenia	...is in the continent of North America. Basseterre is the capital. People are called Kittitians, and on Nevis they are called Nevisians. When Christopher Columbus discovered the island, he named it after his patron saint, St. Christopher. Later the name was shortened to St. Kitts, his nickname.

GROUP DISCUSSION AND CLOSING PRAYER

"Prayer is an acknowledgment that our need of God's help is not partial but total."

Alistair Begg

Day 80 ~ The Judgment on the Nation

Moreover the LORD...

OPENING PRAYER
READ: Isaiah 8:1-21

1) What was the message of warning God told Isaiah to write as a large public sign?_____
_____

2) What instructions were given to Isaiah? _____
_____

3) What were the functions of mediums and wizards?_____
_____

Explore God's World

MEMORY VERSES:

Matthew 5:13-14 "You are the salt of the earth; but if the salt loses its flavor, how shall it be seasoned? It is then good for nothing but to be thrown out and trampled underfoot by men. You are the light of the world. A city that is set on a hill cannot be hidden."

SYNOPSIS OF 2ND CHRONICLES

The book is a narrative history. The author appears to be the prophet Ezra, who wrote it circa 430 B.C. It covers the events from the beginning of King Solomon's reign in 970 B.C. to the beginning of the Babylonian captivity in 586 B.C. The key personalities are King Solomon, the queen of Sheba, Rehoboam, Asa, Jehoshaphat, Jehoram, Joash, Uzziah, Ahaz, Hezekiah, Manasseh, and Josiah. Written to emphasize the blessings of the righteous kings and to chronicle the sins of the wicked kings, the book parallels some parts of 1st and 2nd Kings. Both Chronicles were written from the spiritual perspective of a priest who spoke to the returning exiles by focusing on correct worship of YHWH, the Jewish spelling for Jehovah/God. The book records again the revival under King Josiah.

For Your Information

FUN FACTS	THE SEVEN COUNTRIES WITH THE MOST SUICIDES	SAINT LUCIA
1. There are more vacant houses than homeless people in the United States. 2. Luther Burbank was a plant breeder who developed over 800 new strains of plants, including many popular varieties of Idaho potato, plums, prunes, berries, trees, and flowers.	1) Lithuania 2) Russia 3) Belarus 4) Latvia 5) Estonia 6) Hungary 7) Slovenia	...is in the continent of North America. Castries is the capital. Named after Saint Lucy of Syracuse by the French, the volcanic island is more mountainous than many other Caribbean islands. Its currency is the East Caribbean Dollar (EC$).

GROUP DISCUSSION AND CLOSING PRAYER

"Life isn't about waiting for the storm to pass; it's about learning to dance in the rain."

Vivian Greene

Day 81 ~ The Lord Exhorts Israel

OPENING PRAYER
READ: Isaiah 40:1-23

"Comfort, yes, comfort...

1) What message is found in "the voice of the one crying in the wilderness"?_____
_____

2) What is the difference between grass and the Word of God?_____
_____

3) What lesson can we find in verses 22 and 23? _____
_____

Explore God's World

MEMORY VERSES:
Matthew 5:13-14 "You are the salt of the earth; but if the salt loses its flavor, how shall it be seasoned? It is then good for nothing but to be thrown out and trampled underfoot by men. You are the light of the world. A city that is set on a hill cannot be hidden."

SYNOPSIS OF EZRA
The book is of narrative history and genealogies. It was written by Ezra at approximately 440 B.C. and records events up to 450 B.C. Key personalities include Cyrus, Ezra, Haggai, Zechariah, Darius I, Artaxerxes I, and Zerubbabel. Ezra's purpose was to accurately record the Israelites' return from the Babylonian exile after a 72 year period and the events that surrounded the rebuilding of the temple in Jerusalem. Ezra shows that God is faithful in fulfilling His promises through the Jews' return to Jerusalem from their exile in Babylon.

For Your Information

FUN FACTS	THE SEVEN COUNTRIES WITH THE MOST SUICIDES	SAINT VINCENT AND THE GRENADINES
1. 2.6 million bars of soap are discarded daily by the hotel industry in the U.S. alone. 2. The mechanical cash register was invented in 1879 by James Ritty. He was an American tavern keeper who nicknamed his cash register the "Incorruptible Cashier."	1) Lithuania 2) Russia 3) Belarus 4) Latvia 5) Estonia 6) Hungary 7) Slovenia	...is in the continent of North America. Kingstown is the capital. The parrot is the National Bird. English and Vincentian Creole are the official languages. The country has its own football league and national rugby union team. Agriculture is dominated by banana production.

GROUP DISCUSSION AND CLOSING PRAYER

"The best thing about the future is that it comes one day at a time."

Abraham Lincoln

Day 82 ~ Messiah Brings Light & Restoration

OPENING PRAYER
READ: Isaiah 49:1-26

Listen, O coastlands...

1) When did God place His call on His servant, the Messiah?_____

_____

2) What did God promise to show through his servant?_____

_____

3) What can one learn from God's dealings with Israel's oppressors?_____

_____

Explore God's World

MEMORY VERSES:

Matthew 5:13-14 "You are the salt of the earth; but if the salt loses its flavor, how shall it be seasoned? It is then good for nothing but to be thrown out and trampled underfoot by men. You are the light of the world. A city that is set on a hill cannot be hidden."

SYNOPSIS OF NEHEMIAH
The book is narrative history. Nehemiah authored it at about 430 B.C. Key personalities include Nehemiah, Ezra, Sanballat, and Tobiah. The prophet wrote the book to record the events of the Israelites' returning to Jerusalem and rebuilding the walls in 445 B.C. Jerusalem had a temple but there was no protection for the city from further attack. Nehemiah travels to Jerusalem to rally a citywide construction crew. Within a few weeks, the walls around Jerusalem were built and standing tall and their enemies lost their confidence to attack the city.

For Your Information

FUN FACTS	THE SEVEN COUNTRIES WITH THE MOST SUICIDES	SAMOA
1. "Queueing" is the only word with five consecutive vowels. 2. There is a glacier in Antarctica called "Blood Falls" that regularly pours out red liquid, making the glacier look like the ice is bleeding.	1) Lithuania 2) Russia 3) Belarus 4) Latvia 5) Estonia 6) Hungary 7) Slovenia	...is in the continent of Australia (Oceanic). Apia is the capital. Samoan and English are official languages. Samoans have two gender specific and culturally significant tattoos. Rugby is the national sport. The two main islands are Upolu and Savai'i.

GROUP DISCUSSION AND CLOSING PRAYER

"The greatest and best talent that God gives to any man or woman in this world is the talent of prayer."

Alexander Whyte

Day 83 ~ Messiah will be Filled with the Spirit of the Lord

OPENING PRAYER
READ: Isaiah 61:1-11

The Spirit of the...

1) What are the purposes for which God's anointed was sent into the world?_____
_____

2) How did the work force of Israel reflect its power and status?_____
_____

3) What does God hate?_____
_____

Explore God's World

MEMORY VERSES:

Matthew 5:13-14 "You are the salt of the earth; but if the salt loses its flavor, how shall it be seasoned? It is then good for nothing but to be thrown out and trampled underfoot by men. You are the light of the world. A city that is set on a hill cannot be hidden."

SYNOPSIS OF ESTHER

The genre of the book is narrative history. Its author is anonymous however, some believe Mordecai, Esther's cousin and guardian, wrote it written approximately 470 B.C. in Persia. Esther became queen in 479 B.C. The key personalities are Esther, Mordecai, King Ahasuerus (or Xerxes), and Haman. The book of Esther, which is a post exile story about Jews who stayed behind after most Israelites returned to Jerusalem after the captivity, demonstrates God's love and sovereignty in all circumstances. Babylon was conquered by Persia and Esther miraculously became the queen of the land. Through her courageous act, she saved her people from the diabolical plan of Haman to slay all the Jews. It is one of only two books of the Bible that does not mention God. The other book is the Song of Solomon.

For Your Information

FUN FACTS	THE SEVEN COUNTRIES WITH THE MOST SUICIDES	SAN MARINO
1. In Japan, there are more pets than there are children. 2. Bandages for wounds had been around since ancient times, but Earle Dickson perfected the BAND-AID in 1920 by making a small, sterile adhesive bandage for home use.	1) Lithuania 2) Russia 3) Belarus 4) Latvia 5) Estonia 6) Hungary 7) Slovenia	...is in the continent of Europe. San Marino is the capital. The country is two times smaller than Green Bay, Wisconsin. The main agricultural products are wine and cheese. The San Marino postage stamps are valid for mail only within the country.

GROUP DISCUSSION AND CLOSING PRAYER

"Everybody pities the weak; jealousy you have to earn."
Arnold Schwarzenegger

Day 84 ~ Week in Review

MATCH THE FOLLOWING

_____ a. Saint Vincent and the Grenadines   1. Basseterre

_____ b. Nehemiah   2. San Marino

_____ c. Rwanda   3. History, and Genealogies

_____ d. Samoa   4. Kingstown

_____ e. 2nd Kings   5. Mordecai, King Ahasuerus, and Haman

_____ f. Esther   6. Kigali

_____ g. Saint Kitts and Nevis   7. Rebuilding the walls

_____ h. San Marino   8. Castries

_____ i. 1st Chronicles   9. Apia

_____ j. Saint Lucia   10. History and Prophecy

TRUE OR FALSE — Circle T for true or F for false

T or F   The book of 1st Chronicles was written before the exile.

T or F   Rwanda's major cash crops for export include wheat, rice and sugarcane.

T or F   Saint Lucia is named after Saint Lucy of Syracuse by the French.

T or F   Ezra accurately recorded the events of the return from the Babylonian exile.

T or F   Saint Vincent's national bird is the eagle.

T or F   In Samoa, French, Samoan and English are official languages.

T or F   2nd Kings purpose demonstrates the value of those who obey God.

T or F   San Marino's postage stamps are valid for mail only within the country.

T or F   People of St. Lucia are called Kittitians and on Nevis they are called Nevisians.

T or F   The author of 2nd Chronicles appears to be the prophet Ezra.

LIST THE SEVEN COUNTRIES WITH THE MOST SUICIDES

1. _____   2. _____

3. _____   4. _____

5. _____   6. _____

7. _____

FILL IN THE BLANKS

a. St. Lucia's _____ island is more _____ than many other Caribbean _____ .

b. Nehemiah record the _____ of the Israelites' returning to _____ and re-building the _____ in _____ B.C.

c. Ezra's purpose was to _____ record the _____ return from the _____ Exile.

d. In Rwanda, coffee and _____ are the _____ cash _____ for export.

e. Saint Vincent has its own _____ league and _____ rugby union _____ .

f. San Marino has _____ agricultural _____ which are _____ and _____ .

g. 1st Chronicles relates the _____ given to the _____ that came out of the Babylonian _____ .

h. 2nd Kings is _____ history and _____ concerning the _____ of the divided _____ .

i. Samoans have _____ gender _____ and culturally _____ tattoos.

j. When Christopher Columbus discovered the _____ of Saint Kitts and _____ , he named it _____ his _____ patron saint, St.

MEMORIZE AND WRITE

Matthew 5:13-14 _____

_____

_____

_____

_____

GOD'S LOVE

God does whatever He can to draw us back when we fall away from His path. Name some examples of how Israel fell away from God and what God did to try to draw Israel back to Him. Has God done that in your own life when you have not followed God's best for you?

_____

_____

_____

_____

_____

The Birth of Jesus Coloring Activity

Note, you may make copies of this page to color if multiple family members in the same household want to color the illustration.

Day 85 ~ The Call of Jeremiah

OPENING PRAYER
READ: Jeremiah 1:1-19

The words of Jeremiah...

1) How is Jeremiah indentified at the beginning of the book?_____

_____

2) How did God respond to Jeremiah's uncertainties?_____

_____

3) How did God describe Jeremiah's mission as prophet?_____

_____

Explore God's World

MEMORY VERSES:

Matthew 5:15-16 "Nor do they light a lamp and put it under a basket, but on a lampstand, and it gives light to all who are in the house. Let your light so shine before men, that they may see your good works and glorify your Father in heaven."

SYNOPSIS OF JOB

The book is narrative history. Though the author is unknown, possibly Job, himself, is the writer. Written approximately 2100-1800 B.C., Job is perhaps the oldest of any book of the Bible. Key personalities of this book include Job, Eliphaz the Temanite, Bildad the Shuhite, Zophar the Naamathite, and Elihu the Buzite. In Job, we see a man whom God allowed to be directly attacked by Satan. Though he lost material possessions and all his children and was himself stricken with physical pain and misery, he remained faithful to God. The narrative illustrates God's sovereignty and justice by rewarding Job doubly for his faithfulness during a time of great suffering.

For Your Information

FUN FACTS	THE SEVEN COUNTRIES WITH THE LARGEST FORESTS	SÃO TOMÉ AND PRÍNCIPE
1. There are 13 ways to spell the "O" sound in French. 2. Piranhas are fish that are cannibals. They will attack and eat other piranhas during a frenzied state or even in an underfed state.	1) Russia 2) Brazil 3) Canada 4) USA 5) China 6) Australia 7) Democratic Republic of the Congo	...are an island nation in the continent of Africa. Sao Tome is the capital. The country has the 2nd smallest population in the world. The nation is home to a large number of birds and plants, including the world's smallest ibis, the world's largest sunbird, and a giant species of begonia. Staple foods include fish, seafood, beans, maize, and cooked banana.

GROUP DISCUSSION AND CLOSING PRAYER

"Good people do not need laws to tell them to act responsibly, while bad people will find a way around the laws.."

Plato

Day 86 ~ The Broken Covenant

OPENING PRAYER
READ: Jeremiah 11:1-13 and 12:1-12

The word that came...

1) Why was God going to punish His people? _____

_____

2) What questions concerning God's justice did Jeremiah pose to God? _____

_____

3) How did the Lord answer Jeremiah? _____

_____

Explore God's World

MEMORY VERSES:

Matthew 5:15-16 "Nor do they light a lamp and put it under a basket, but on a lampstand, and it gives light to all who are in the house. Let your light so shine before men, that they may see your good works and glorify your Father in heaven."

SYNOPSIS OF PSALMS

The genre of Psalms consists of songs and poetry of all kinds written by multiple authors: David wrote 73, Asaph wrote 12, the sons of Korah wrote 9, Solomon wrote 3, Ethan, and Moses each wrote one (Ps. 90), and 51 of the Psalms are anonymous. Beginning at the time of Moses 1440 B.C., and through the captivity in 586 B.C., they were written over the span of approximately 900 years. The Psalms communicated praises of joy, blessings, thanksgivings, and laments to God. The psalmist's emotions ranged from one extreme to another; from praising, delighting in, and worshiping God with fervor to repentance and crying out to Him in despair.

For Your Information

FUN FACTS	THE SEVEN COUNTRIES WITH THE LARGEST FORESTS	SAUDI ARABIA
1. Japan's birth rate is so low that more adult diapers are sold than baby diapers. 2. In ancient Egypt, servants were smeared with honey to attract flies away from the pharaoh.	1) Russia 2) Brazil 3) Canada 4) USA 5) China 6) Australia 7) Democratic Republic of the Congo	...is in the continent of Asia. Riyadh is the capital. Women under 45 cannot travel alone without a specific form or an electronic authorization. Saudi Arabia has the world's 2nd largest oil reserves and the world's 6th largest natural gas reserves.

GROUP DISCUSSION AND CLOSING PRAYER

"The prayer that begins with trustfulness, and passes on into waiting, will always end in thankfulness, triumph, and praise."

Alexander MacLaren

Day 87 ~ Jeremiah's Lament Over the Nation

OPENING PRAYER

READ: Jeremiah 14:1-16 and 15:19-21

Then Samuel died...

1) What desperate situation did Jeremiah predict for Jerusalem?_____

_____

2) What do we learn from verses 14-15 about prophets?_____

_____

3) What promise did God make to His servant, Jeremiah?_____

_____

Explore God's World

MEMORY VERSES:

Matthew 5:15-16 "Nor do they light a lamp and put it under a basket, but on a lampstand, and it gives light to all who are in the house. Let your light so shine before men, that they may see your good works and glorify your Father in heaven."

SYNOPSIS OF PROVERBS

The genre of the book is mainly "proverbs" as the name indicates, but also includes some parables and poetry. This book was written mainly by Solomon, the wisest king ever to rule; however, some of the later sections were written by Lemuel and Agur. Some people think Lemuel is a pen name for Solomon. It was written during Solomon's reign 970-930 B.C. He requested of God to be given wisdom to rule the chosen nation. The main purpose of this book is to teach wisdom to God's people. The succinct proverbial statements contain truisms which are typically true, but not always. For example, "He who tills his land will have plenty of bread" (12:11) is not a guarantee that is always true. The nuggets of wisdom addressing life, principles, good judgment, and perception often draw distinctions between a wise man and a foolish man.

For Your Information

FUN FACTS	THE SEVEN COUNTRIES WITH THE LARGEST FORESTS	SENEGAL
1. All of the bacteria in the human body collectively weighs about 4 pounds. 2. Alessandro Volta invented the first chemical battery in 1800. The non-acid alkaline batteries are an improved type of storage battery developed by Thomas Edison.	1) Russia 2) Brazil 3) Canada 4) USA 5) China 6) Australia 7) Democratic Republic of the Congo	...is in the continent of Africa. Dakar is the capital. The previous capital was St. Louis. The climate is tropical with a dry and a rainy season. Cotton, fabrics, ground nuts, fish, chemicals, and calcium phosphate are the country's exports.

GROUP DISCUSSION AND CLOSING PRAYER

"The only difference between me and a madman is that I'm not mad."

Salvador Dali

Day 88 ~ A Sign of Two Baskets of Figs

OPENING PRAYER
READ: Jeremiah 24:1-10

The LORD showed...

1) Which inhabitants of Judah were taken into exile in Babylon?_____

_____

2) What gift did God promise to the exiles? _____

_____

3) What did God intend to send against king of Judah?_____

_____

Explore God's World

MEMORY VERSES:

Matthew 5:15-16 "Nor do they light a lamp and put it under a basket, but on a lampstand, and it gives light to all who are in the house. Let your light so shine before men, that they may see your good works and glorify your Father in heaven."

SYNOPSIS OF ECCLESIASTES

The book contains proverbs, maxims, and sayings is largely an autobiographical story of Solomon, who wrote it late in his life, approximately 935 BC. He had become aware of the mistakes that he made throughout his life and began to document them: "I set my mind to seek and explore by wisdom concerning all that has been done under heaven. It is a grievous task which God has given to the sons of men to be afflicted with" (1:13). The purpose of Ecclesiastes is to spare future generations the suffering and misery of seeking after foolish, meaningless, materialistic emptiness, and to offer wisdom by discovering truth in seeking after God.

For Your Information

FUN FACTS	THE SEVEN COUNTRIES WITH THE LARGEST FORESTS	SERBIA
1. The song "Jingle Bells" was written for Thanksgiving. 2. A metal can (or canister) for preserving food was invented in 1810 by a Peter Durand of London, England. While the can opener was invented in 1858 by Ezra Warner.	1) Russia 2) Brazil 3) Canada 4) USA 5) China 6) Australia 7) Democratic Republic of the Congo	...is in the continent of Europe. Belgrade is the capital. The clock-making industry in Serbia is even older than the world-famous Swiss one. Serbia had its own clock 600 years before the Swiss. Constantine the Great, the Roman Emperor, was Serbian.

GROUP DISCUSSION AND CLOSING PRAYER

"Prayer that runs its course till the last day of life needs a strong and tranquil soul."

Clement of Alexandria

Day 89 ~ Judah & the Nations

OPENING PRAYER
READ: Jeremiah 25:1-29

The word that...

1) What was the message from God to the people of Judah and Jerusalem? _____
_____

2) How did the people bring God's judgment on themselves? _____
_____

3) Where did David send some of the spoil? _____
_____

Explore God's World

MEMORY VERSES:

Matthew 5:15-16 "Nor do they light a lamp and put it under a basket, but on a lampstand, and it gives light to all who are in the house. Let your light so shine before men, that they may see your good works and glorify your Father in heaven."

SYNOPSIS OF SONG OF SOLOMON

The book is a large love poem filled with smaller poems of different kinds. Solomon wrote it during his reign from 970-930 B.C. The story is of a bridegroom who is in love with his bride. Key personalities are King Solomon, the Shulammite girl, and friends. The story greatly emphasizes the sanctity of marriage which God designed, blessed, and consecrated. The purpose of "Song of Songs," as it is also called, pictures God's love for His people. Although there is explicit sexual content, the book depicts the depths of God's authentic love for us through the sacredness of marriage. It is one of two books in the Bible that do not mention God. The other is the Book of Esther.

For Your Information

FUN FACTS	THE SEVEN COUNTRIES WITH THE LARGEST FORESTS	SEYCHELLES
1. An individual banana is called a finger. A bunch of bananas is called a hand. 2. The location of the world's tallest tree, "Hyperion," is kept secret from all but a few scientists.	1) Russia 2) Brazil 3) Canada 4) USA 5) China 6) Australia 7) Democratic Republic of the Congo	...is in the continent of Africa. Victoria is the capital. Seychelles has no indigenous population. The country is an archipelago of 115 islands in the Indian Ocean off East Africa, known for its beaches, coral reefs, diving, nature reserves and rare wildlife such as the giant Aldabra tortoises. The official languages of Seychelles are French, English, and Seselwa.

GROUP DISCUSSION AND CLOSING PRAYER

"Dancing is silent poetry."

Simonides

Day 90 ~ *The Fall of Jerusalem*

OPENING PRAYER
READ: Jeremiah 52:1-30

Zedekiah was twenty-one...

1) How did God view Zedekiah, king of Judah?_____

_____

2) What was Zedekiah's punishment for rebelling against Babylon?_____

_____

3) Why did Nebuchadnezzar lay siege to the city of Jerusalem and what happened to the temple?_____

_____

Explore God's World

MEMORY VERSES:
Matthew 5:15-16

"Nor do they light a lamp and put it under a basket, but on a lampstand, and it gives light to all who are in the house. Let your light so shine before men, that they may see your good works and glorify your Father in heaven."

SYNOPSIS OF ISAIAH

The book is narrative history, prophetic oracle, and even a parable (chapter 5). The prophet Isaiah wrote chapters 1-39 approximately 700 B.C., while chapters 40-66 were written later in his life, about 681 B.C. Isaiah is the first book in the section called the Major Prophets; so-called because of the large amount of material, not because the message was more important than any other prophet's. Key personalities are Isaiah, and his two sons, Shearjashub and Maher-shalal-jash-baz. Of all prophecy books, Isaiah contains incredible details about the coming Messiah "Immanuel" and the future reign of Jesus Christ. God commissions His prophet to pronounce condemnation on Judah and Israel for their sins, to call them to repentance, and to promise the nation's ultimate, future restoration.

For Your Information

FUN FACTS	THE SEVEN COUNTRIES WITH THE LARGEST FORESTS	SIERRA LEONE
1. Central Africa holds the record for the highest twin birthrate, with an average of 27.9 twins per 1,000 births. 2. Cats have scent glands in the paws, When they knead their pawns into us, they are marking their territory.	1) Russia 2) Brazil 3) Canada 4) USA 5) China 6) Australia 7) Democratic Republic of the Congo	…is in the continent of Africa. Freetown is the capital. The country made headlines on 14 February 1972, when the "Star of Sierra Leone," the third largest gem-quality diamond in the world, was discovered in Koidu.

GROUP DISCUSSION AND CLOSING PRAYER

"Try to learn something about everything and everything about something."

Thomas Henry Huxley

Day 91 ~ Week in Review

MEMORIZE AND WRITE

Matthew 5:15-16_____

_____

_____

TRUE OR FALSE — Circle T for true or F for false

T or F   Solomon wrote Ecclesiastes when he was young and had many teachers.

T or F   Senegal's climate is a mild winter with strong winds.

T or F   Constantine the Great, the Roman Emperor, was Serbian.

T or F   Saudi Arabian woman have all the equal rights as their men.

T or F   Song of Solomon's purpose was to get rich through learning wisdom.

T or F   In Job, we see a man who God allows to be directly attacked by Satan.

T or F   Solomon's wisdom came as he started writing the Proverbs.

T or F   Isaiah declares the coming Messiah "Immanuel".

T or F   The Psalms include praises of joy, laments, blessings, and thanksgivings.

T or F   Sierra Leone is the 3rd largest gem-quality diamond in the world was discovered.

MATCH THE FOLLOWING

_____ a. Senegal   1. Sao Tome

_____ b. Sierra Leone   2. Parables and Poetry

_____ c. Psalms   3. Belgrade

_____ d. Song of Solomon   4. History and Unknown

_____ e. Sao Tome and Principe   5. Freetown

_____ f. Isaiah   6. Riyadh

_____ g. Seychelles   7. Proverbs, maxims and sayings

_____ h. Ecclesiastes   8. Love poem

_____ i. Saudi Arabia   9. Dakar

_____ j. Proverbs   10. Songs and Poetry

_____ k. Job   10. Victoria

_____ l. Serbia   10. Prophetic Oracle and a Parable

LIST THE SEVEN COUNTRIES WITH LARGEST FORESTS

1. _____   2. _____

3. _____   4. _____

5. _____   6. _____

7. _____

FILL IN THE BLANKS

a. Senegal exports Cotton, fabrics, ground nuts,_____, chemicals, and calcium_____.

b. Ecclesiastes contains _____, maxims,_____, and is largely an_____story.

c. The main _____of Proverbs is to_____wisdom to God's_____.

d. Isaiah contains_____details about the coming_____"Immanuel" and the reign of _____ _____.

e. Serbia had its own clock_____years before the_____.

f. The official _____of Seychelles is French, _____, and_____.

g. Psalms communicated praises of_____, blessings,_____, and laments to_____.

h. Song of Solomon is a_____love_____filled with_____poems of _____kinds.

i. Saudi Arabia has the_____2nd_____oil_____and the world's_____ largest natural _____reserves.

UNCERTAINTIES

Like Jeremiah, each of us face uncertainties, especially about what we are supposed to do for the Lord each day. What are some uncertainties you have faced or are facing now, and how can you use the example of Jeremiah to find confidence in the path God has for you?

_____

_____

_____

_____

_____

ACTIVITY: ON A BLANK PIECE OF PAPER, DRAW A T-GRAPH. ON ONE SIDE OF THE GRAPH, LIST THE THINGS YOU ARE CURRENTLY UNCERTAIN ABOUT IN YOUR-LIFE, THEN ON THE OTHER SIDE, LIST THE THINGS YOU KNOW FOR SURE THAT GOD WANTS YOU TO DO (*Keep in mind that some simple things we can be sure God wants us to do include reaching others for christ, but be sure you list where you can specifically do that*).

Things I am uncertain about	Things I know God wants me to do

GLOSSARY & REFERENCES

A

Abbreviated—[uh-bree-vee-ey-tid] To shorten or reduce (anything) in length.

Aboriginal—[ab-uh-rij-uh-nl] Original or earliest known; native; indigenous.

Accumulation—[uh-kyoo-myuh-ley-shuh n] Something that has been collected, gathered.

Admonished—[ad-mon-ish] To caution, advise, or counsel against something.

Ancient—Dating from a remote period; of great age.

Adulterous—Unfaithful

Alleviate—[uh-lee-vee-eyt] lighten, easier to bear, relieve.

Anonymous—uh-non-uh-muh s] Without any name acknowledged, as that of author or Contributor.

Apocalyptic—[uh-pok-uh-lip-tik] Predicting an imminent disaster or universal destruction.

Apokalupsis—[uh-pok-uh-lips] Any revelation or prophecy.

Apostolic—[ap-uh-stol-ik] Pertaining to or characteristic of the 12 Apostles.

Archipelago—[ahr-kuh-pel-uh-goh] Any large body of water with many islands.

Asceticism—[uh-set-uh-siz uh m] The doctrine that a person can attain a high spiritual and moral state by practicing self-denial, self-mortification, and the like.

Asymmetrical—[ey-suh-me-trik, as-uh-] not identical on both sides of a central line, unsymmetrical.

Atonement—The reconciliation of man with God through the life, sufferings, and sacrificial death of Jesus Christ

Atrocities—[uh-tros-i-tee] Behaviour or an action that is wicked or ruthless.

Autobiographical—Marked by or dealing with one's own experiences or life history.

Autopsy—[aw-top-see] inspection of a body after death, as for determination of the cause of death.

B

Beethoven—German composer (1770–1827)

Beetle—Any of various insects resembling the beetle, as a cockroach.

Bosom—The breast of a human being.

Botany—The branch of biology that deals with plant life.

C

Camouflage—[kam-uh-flahzh] As by painting or screening objects so that they are lost lost to view in theback-ground.

Cannibals—Any animal that eats its own kind.

Cays—A small low Island

Cerinthianism—A heresy taught that deals with the person of Jesus.

Cessation—[se-sey-shuh n] a temporary or complete stopping; discontinuance.

Chronicles—A record or register of events in chronological order

Chronological—A sequence of events, arranged in order of occurrence.

Circumcision—The rite of circumcising, spiritual purification.

Circumspect—[sur-*kuh* m-spekt] watchful and discreet; cautious; prudent.

Colosseum—An ancient amphitheater in Rome, begun AD 70.

Commencement—[*kuh*-mens-*muh* nt] To Begin.

Compulsory—[*kuh* m-puhl-*suh*-ree] Required; mandatory; obligatory.

Conclusive—[*kuh* n-kloo-siv] Serving to settle or decide a question; decisive; convincing.

Condemnation—[kon-dem-ney-sh*uh* n, -*duh* m-] To pronounce to be guilty, sentence to punishment.

Contemplating—To consider thoroughly.

Contending—To struggle in opposition:

Continent—The mainland, as distinguished from islands or peninsulas.

Conservation—[kon-ser-vey-sh*uh* n] The careful utilization of a natural resource in order to prevent depletion.

Consistent—[*kuh* n-sis-t*uh* nt] Agreeing or accordant; compatible; not self-contradictory.

Conspiracy—[*kuh* n-spir-*uh*-see] A combination of persons for a secret, unlawful or evil purpose.

Cortex—The outer region of an organ or structure, as the outer portion of the kidney.

Covenant—An oath or agreement, deed.

Cumulative—[kyoo-my*uh*-luh-tiv, -ley-tiv] growing in quantity, strength, or effect.

Cymbals—[sim bah l] A concave plate of brass or bronze that produces a sharp, ringing sound when struck.

D

Decay—To decline in excellence, prosperity, health, etc.

Deforestation—The cutting down and removal of all or most of the trees in a forested area.

Decimated—[des-*uh*-meyt] To destroy or kill a large proportion of: *a plague.*

Deities—A god or goddess.

Delicacy—[del-i-*kuh*-see] something delightful or pleasing, especially a choice considered with regard to its rarity.

Depravity—To make morally bad or evil; vitiate; corrupt.

Deliverance—To set free or release.

Deportation—The lawful expulsion of an undesired alien or other person from a state.

Descendants—A person or animal that is descended from a specific ancestor; an offspring.

Desertification—[dih-zur-t*uh*-fi-key-sh*uh* n] A process by which fertile land turns into barren land or desert.

Detection—To discover or catch (a person) in the performance of some act.

Derived—To trace from a source or origin.

Deuteronomy—[doo-t*uh*-ron-*uh*-mee, dyoo-] The 5th book in the Bible.

Dictatorial—Appropriate to, or characteristic of, a dictator; absolute; unlimited: dictatorial power in wartime.

Differentiate—To form or mark differently from other such things; distinguish.

Diligently—Constant in effort to accomplish something.

Diotrephes—A man mentioned in the Third Epistle of John (verses 9–11). His name means "nourished by Jupiter."

Disciplinary—Training to act in accordance with rules; drill.

Distorted—[dih-stawr-tid] not truly or completely representing the facts or reality; misrepresented; false.

Docetism—[doh-see-tiz-*uh* m, doh-si-tiz] A early Christian doctrine that the sufferings of Christ were apparent and not real and that after the crucifixion He appeared in a spiritual body.

Doctrines—A particular principle, position, or policy taught or advocated, as of a religion or government.

Drought—A period of dry weather, especially a long one that is injurious to crops.

E

Ecclesiastes—[ih-klee-zee-as-teez] A book of the Bible.

Economy—thrifty management; thoughtful or wise in spending resources.

Elixirs—[ih-lik-ser] A sweetened aromatic solution of alcohol and water serving as a vehicle for medicine.

Elohim—[e-loh-him] God, especially as used in the Hebrew text of the Old Testament.

Emerges—To rise or come forth from or as if from water or other liquid.

Emphasis—Something that is given great stress or importance.

Ensues—To follow in order; come afterward, especially in immediate succession.

Entrepreneur—[ahn-truh-pruh-nur] A person who organizes and manages any enterprise, especially a business.

Epistle—A letter, especially a formal or instructive one.

Exaltation—Raise or elevate, as in rank or character; of high station.

Exclusion—[ik-skloo-zhuh n] To shut or keep out; prevent the entrance of.

Exodus—A going out; a departure or emigration, usually ofa large number of people.

Exile—To expel or banish (a person) from his or her country.

Explicitly—Precisely and clearly expressed, leaving nothing to implication; fully stated.

Exporter—To ship (commodities) to other countries or placesfor sale, exchange, etc.

F

Fending off —To try to prevent something.

Forensic—[fuh-ren-sik] The art or study of argumentation and formal debate.

Forewarned—[fawr-wawrn, foh] To warn in advance.

Francophone—[frang-kuh-fohn] A person who speaks French, especially a native speak.

Frenzied—[fren-zeed] Wildly excited or enthusiastic.

Frontlets—[fruhnt-lit] A decorative band, ribbon, or the like, worn across the forehead.

Futility—[fyoo-til-i-tee] The quality of being futile; ineffectiveness; uselessness.

G

Genealogical—[jee-nee-ol-uh-jee, -al-, jen-ee-] A record or account of the ancestry and descent of a person, family, group, etc.

Gentile—[jen-tahyl] A person who is not Jewish, especially a Christian.

Genres—A class or category of artistic endeavor having a particular form, content, technique, or the like the genre of epic poetry; the genre of symphonic music.

GDP—Gross domestic product.

Gnostic—[nos-tik] Pertaining to knowledge.

H

Hedonism—[heed-n-iz-uh m] the doctrine that pleasure or happiness is the highest good.

Heresy—[her-uh-see] Opinion or doctrine at variance with the orthodox or accepted doctrine, especially of a church or religious system.

Holocaust—[hol-uh-kawst] A great or complete devastation or destruction, especially by fire.

Hymnal—[him-nl] A book of hymns/songs for use in a religious service.

Hypocrites—[hip-uh-krit] A person who pretends to have virtues, moral or religious beliefs, priniciples.

I

Idolatrous—[ahy-dol-uh-truh s] Worshiping idols.

IMF—The International Monetary Fund.

Immense—Vast; huge; very great

Immorality—[im-*uh*-ral-i-tee] Immoral character, or conduct; wickedness; evilness.

Impending—About to happen; imminent.

Importer—To bring in (merchandise, commodities, workers,etc.) from a foreign country for use, sale,processing, reexport, or services.

Imputation—[im-pyoo-tey-sh*uh* n] An attribution, as of fault or crime; accusation.

Indigenous—[in-dij-*uh*-nuh s] Originating in and characteristic of a particular region or country; native.

Inevitable—[in-ev-i-t*uh*-b*uh* l] Unable to be avoided, evaded, or escaped; certain; necessary.

Ingredient—[in-gree-dee-*uh* nt]Something that enters as an element into a mixture.

Inhabitants—[nˈhæb ɪ tənt/] A person or animal that inhabits a place, especially as a permanent reside.

Intercessory—[in-ter-ses-*uh*-ree] To act or interpose in behalf of someone in difficulty or trouble, as by pleading or petition.

Intertwined—[ɪn tərˈtwaɪn] To twine together.

Insane—Not sane; not of sound mind; mentally deranged.

Itinerant—[ahy-tin-er-*uh* nt, ih-tin-] A person who travels from place to place, especially for duty or business.

J

Justification—A reason, fact, circumstance, or explanation that justifies or defends.

K

Kaffirs—The word is derived from the Arabic term kafir (meaning 'disbeliever'), which originally had the meaning 'one without religion.

L

Lamentations—[lam-*uh* n-tey-sh*uh* n] The book of the Bible in the OT.

Landlocked—Shut in completely, or almost completely by land.

Latin—An Italic language spoken in ancient Rome.

Langur (the golden)—An Old World monkey found in a small region of western Assam, India and in the neighboring foothills of the Black Mountains of Bhutan.

Legalism—Strict adherence, or the principle of strict adherence, to law or prescription

Leviticus—[lɪˈvɪt ɪ kəs] The third book of the Bible, containing laws relating to the priests and Levites and to the forms of Jewish ceremonial observance.

Licentiousness—[/laɪˈsɛn ʃəs/] Going beyond customary or proper bounds or limits; disregarding rules.

Linguistic—[/lɪŋˈgwɪs tɪk/] Of or belonging to language.

Lyres—[laɪər] A musical instrument of ancient Greece consisting of a sound box made typically from a turtle shell, with two curved arms connected by a yoke from which strings are stretched to the body, used especially to accompany singing and recitation.

M

Mammals—Any animal of the Mammalia, a large class of warm-blooded vertebrates having mammary glands in the female, a thoracic diaphragm, and a four-chambered heart. The class includes the whales, carnivores, rodents, bats.

Manual—Done, operated, worked, etc., by the hand or hands.

Maxims—A principle or rule of conduct.

Metaphor—A figure of speech in which a term or phrase is applied to something to which it is not literally applicable in order to suggest a resemblance.

Meticulous—[mə'tɪk yə ləs] Taking or showing extreme care about minute details; precise; thorough.

Merchant—[mɜr tʃənt] A person who buys and sells commodities for profit; dealer trader.

Microcredit—The lending of very small amounts of money at low interest, especially to a start-up company or self-employed person.

Monarchy—[mon-er-kee] A state or nation in which the supreme power is actually or nominally lodged in a monarch.

Monotonous—[m*uh*-not-n-*uh* s] Characterizing a sound continuing on one note.

Morality—Conformity to the rules of right conduct; moral or virtuous conduct.

Mozart—Austrian composer (1756–91)

Mundane—Common; ordinary; banal; unimaginative.

Multitude—A great number of people gathered together; crowd.

N

Narrative—[nær ə tɪv] A story or account of events, experiences, or the like, whether true or fictitious.

Nebuchadnezzar—[neb-*uh*-*kuh* d-nez-er, neb-yoo-] A king of Babylonia.

Nutritional—The act or process of nourishing or of being nourished.

O

Obscured—[*uh* b-skyoo r] Not clear to the understanding; hard to perceive.

Odor—The property of a substance that activates the sense of smell.

Oracle—[awr-*uh*-*kuh* l] The agency or medium giving such responses.

Origami—[awr-i-gah-mee] The traditional Japanese art or technique of folding paper into a variety or decorative or representational forms, as of animals or flowers.

p

Pagan—One of a people or community observing a polytheistic religion, as the ancient Romans and Greeks. (No longer in technical use.)

Papyrus—[p*uh*-pahy-r*uh* s] A material on which to write, prepared from thin strips of the pith of this plant laid together, soaked, pressed, and dried, used by the ancient Egyptians, Greeks, and Romans.

Parables—A statement or comment that conveys a meaning indirectly by the use of comparison, analogy, or the like.

Permissive—[per-mis-iv] Habitually or characteristically accepting or tolerant of something, as social behavior orlinguistic usage, that others might disapprove orforbid.

Perplexity—[pər'plɛk sɪ ti] A tangled, involved, or confused condition or situation.

Persistent—[per-sis-t*uh* nt] constantly repeated; continued.

Perspectives—[per-spek-tiv] A technique of depicting volumes and spatial relationships on a flat surface.

Persuaded—[per-sweyd] To prevail on (a person) to do something, as by advising or urging.

Piranhas—Any of several small South American freshwater fishes of the genus Serrasalmus that eat other fish and sometimes plants but occasionally also attack humans and other large animals that enter the water.

Phosphate—[fɒs feɪt] A carbonated drink of water and fruit syrup containing a little phosphoric acid.

Physiologist—[fiz-ee-ol-*uh*-jist] the branch of biology dealing with the functional and activities of living organisms and their parts including all physical and chemical processes

Plague—An epidemic disease that causes high mortality, pestilence.

Plunge—To cast or thrust forcibly or suddenly into something, as a liquid, a penetrable substance, a place, etc.; immerse; submerge.

Polyglot—Knowing or speaking different languages.

Polytheistic—The doctrine that there is more than one god or many gods.

Populous—[pop-*yuh*-*luh* s] Full of residents or inhabitants, as a region; heavily populated.

Principalities—The position or authority of a prince or chief ruler, sovereignty; supreme power.

Predominantly—Having ascendancy, power, authority, or influence over others; preeminent.

Preeminence—Eminent above or before others; superior; surpassing.

Protestant—Any Western Christian who is not an adherent of a Catholic, Anglican, or Eastern Church.

Punitive—[pyoo-ni-tiv] Serving for, concerned with, or inflicting punishment.

R

Radiolucent—[rey-dee-oh-loo-*suh* nt] almost transparent to electromagnetic radiation, esp X-rays.

Rapture—The carrying of a person to another place or sphere of existence.

Rectangular—Having one or more right angles.

Redemption—Theology. deliverance from sin; salvation.

Remonstrance—[ri-mon-str*uh* ns] To say or plead in protest, objection, or disapproval.

Renaissance—[ren-*uh*-sahns] The activity, spirit, or time of the great revival of art, literature, and learning in Europe beginning in the 14th century and extending to the 17th century.

Resumption—[ri-*zuh*mp-sh*uh* n] To go on or continue after interruption.

Revitalizing—[ree-vahyt-l-ahyz] To give new life to.

Riddles—A puzzling question, problem, or matter.

S

Sacredness—Devoted or dedicated to a deity or to some religious purpose; consecrated.

Sane—Having a sound, healthy mind.

Sanskrit—[san-skrit] An Indo European, Indic language, in use since c. 1200 b.c. as the religious and classical literary language of India.

Scrolls—A roll of parchment, paper, copper, or other material, especially one with writing on it: roll of parchment, paper, copper, or other material, especially one with writing on it.

Significant—[sig-nif-i-k*uh* nt] Important; of consequence.

Smeared—To spread or daub an oily, greasy, viscous, or wet substance on.

Sovereign—[sov-rin, sov-er-in, *suhv*-] A person who has supreme power or authority.

Sovereignty—The status, dominion, power, or authority of a sovereign.

Species—A class of individuals having some common characteristics or qualities.

Strand—To leave helpless, as without transport or money, etc

Strenuous—[stren-yoo-*uh* s] Requiring or involving the use of great energy or effort.

Subsequent—[*suh*b-si-kw*uh* nt] Occurring or coming later or after.

Successor—A person or thing that follows, esp a person whosucceeds another in an office.

Superlative—The highest kind, quality, or order; surpassing allelse or others; supreme; extreme.

Sushi—A type of food preparation originating in Japan, consisting of cooked vinegared rice combined with other ingredients such as raw seafood, vegetables and sometimes tropical fruits.

Sutures—[soocher] A joining of the lips or edges of a wound or the like by stitching or some similar process.

Sworn—Having taken an oath.

Synagogues—[sin-*uh*-gog,-gawg] A Jewish house of worship, often having facilities for religious instruction.

Synoptic—[si-nop-tik] Of the 4 Gospels presenting the narrative of Christ's life and ministry.

Synopsis—[si-nop-sis] A brief summary of the plot of a novel, motion picture, play, etc.

T

Theocracy—[thee-ok-*ruh*-see] A form of government in which God or a deity is recognized as the supreme civil ruler.

Theocratic— [thee-*uh*-krat-ik] The Rule of God which serves as a supreme law.

Theological—[thee-*uh*-loj-i-k*uh* l] Based upon the nature and will of God as revealed to humans.

Transfiguration—[trans-fig-y*uh*-rey-sh*uh* n] To change so as to glorify or exalt.

Transgression—[trans-gresh-*uh* n, tranz-] To break or breach of a law, etc; sin or crime.

Treachery—[trech-*uh*-ree] violation of faith; betrayal of trust.

Truisms—A self-evident, obvious truth.

Tychicus—[tɪtʃikəs/] Accompanied the Apostle Paul on a part of his missionary journey.

U

UAE—United Arab Emirates, and its capital is Abu Dhabi.

Unheeded—Disregard, ignore.

V

Vindicated—[vin-di-keyt] To clear, as from an accusation, imputation,suspicion, or the like.

W

Wanderings—Moving from place to place without a fixed plan;

Wages—Earnings, emolument, compensation,

Wrought—[rawt] Not rough or crude.

Y

Ylang-ylang—[ee-lahng-ee-lahng] An aromatic tree, Cananga odorata, of the annona family, native to the Philippines, Java, etc, having fragrant, drooping flowers that yield a volatile oil used in perfumery.

Z

Zephaniah—[zef-*uh*-nahy-*uh*] A book of the Bible bearing his name.

Zoroastrians—One of the world's oldest monotheistic religions emerged from a common prehistoric Indo-Iranian religious system dating to the early 2nd BC.

References

www.mapsofworld.com

www.gotquestions.org/Book

www.wikipedia.org

www.cia.gov/library/publications/the-world-factbook

www.biblegateway.com

CPSIA information can be obtained
at www.ICGtesting.com
Printed in the USA
BVHW06s1042240718
522455BV00002B/3/P

9 781946 174062